Maths

Age 5-6

Contents

Activities

Quick Tests

Paul Broadbent and Peter Patilla

Numbers to 10

Look at these numbers and say them out loud.

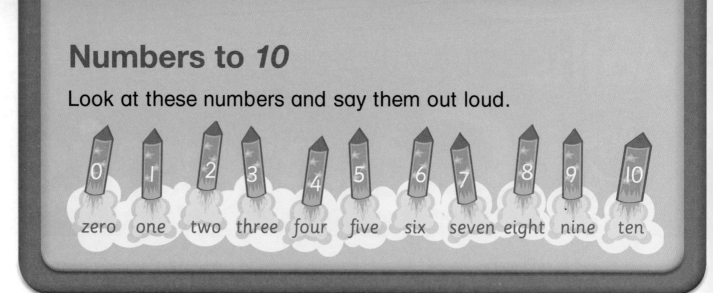

| 0 | 1 | 2 | 3 | 4 | 5 | 6 | 7 | 8 | 9 | 10 |
| zero | one | two | three | four | five | six | seven | eight | nine | ten |

1 Draw over the numbers. Join each one to its matching picture.

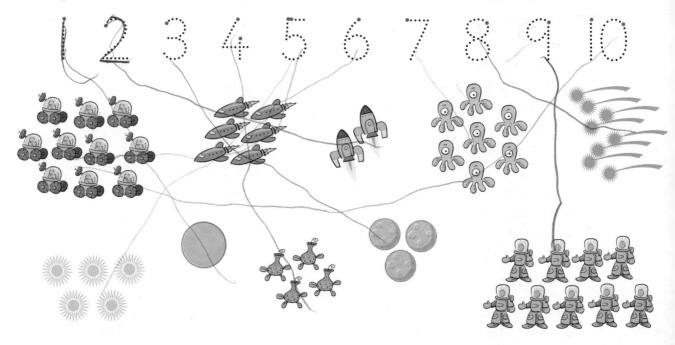

2 Write the number on each planet to match each word.

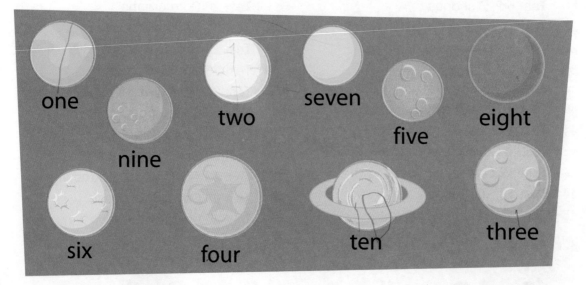

one two seven eight

nine five

six four ten three

2

Counting

Count the shells and say the numbers out loud.

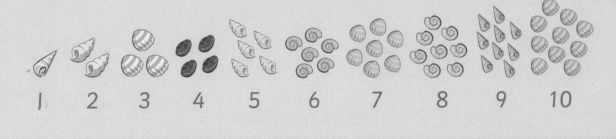

| 1 | 2 | 3 | 4 | 5 | 6 | 7 | 8 | 9 | 10 |

1 Count the things in each group. Write the number.

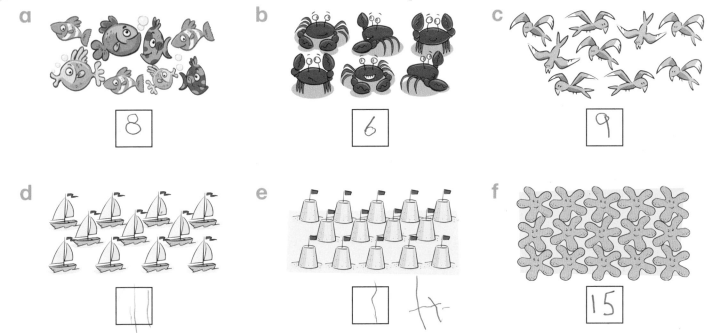

a

8

b

6

c

9

d

11

e

1

f

15

2 Draw 10 more fish in the pool.

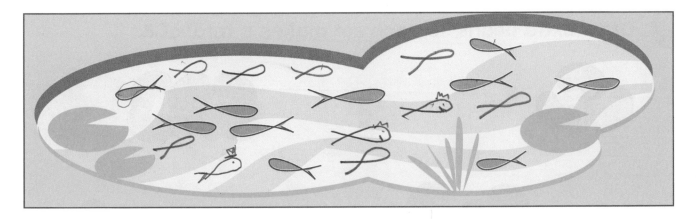

There are 20 fish altogether.

Finding totals

When you **add** sets of objects together, you are finding the total.

4 and 2 makes a total of 6

Count the cars to check the answer.

1 **Find these totals.**

a

3 and 2 makes a total of 5

b

5 and 3 makes a total of 8

c

☐ and ☐ makes a total of ☐

2 **Draw extra beans so each set makes a total of 8.**

8

2-D shapes

Look around you for these 2-D shapes. Try to remember their names.

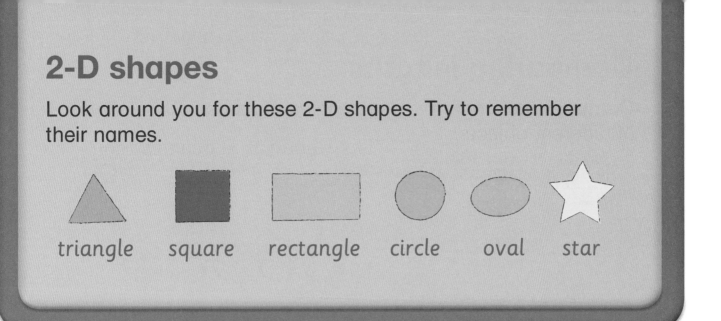

triangle   square   rectangle   circle   oval   star

1 Colour the shapes to match the code. Count the number of each shape.

Number of shapes

2 Draw lines to join each shape to its name.

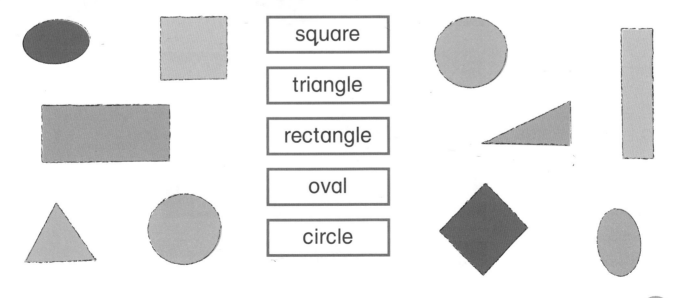

square

triangle

rectangle

oval

circle

Comparing lengths

Compare the lengths of different objects.

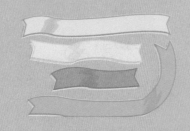

Use pennies to measure the lengths.

This ribbon is 5 pennies long.

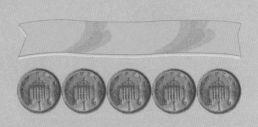

1 Look at these objects.

a Circle the longest in each group.

b Circle the shortest in each group.

2 Measure these lines using pennies.

a ☐ pennies

b ☐ pennies

c ☐ pennies

d ☐ pennies

e ☐ pennies

O'clock time

When the long minute hand points to 12, it is an **o'clock time**.

On a digital clock, an o'clock time ends with **00**.

This is 4 o'clock.

1 Write the time shown on each clock.

a

☐ o'clock

b

☐ o'clock

c

☐ o'clock

d

☐ o'clock

e

☐ o'clock

f

☐ o'clock

g

☐ o'clock

h

☐ o'clock

2 Here are some activities Jack does each Saturday.
Show the time he finishes each of them.

a

start → 1 hour → finish

c

start → 2 hours → finish

b

start → 3 hours → finish

d

start → 1 hour → finish

Numbers to 20

Look at these numbers and say them out loud.

11 eleven	14 fourteen	17 seventeen	20 twenty
12 twelve	15 fifteen	18 eighteen	
13 thirteen	16 sixteen	19 nineteen	

1 Draw over each number, starting at the red dot.

11   12   16   17

14   13   18   19

15   20

2 Write the number to match each word.

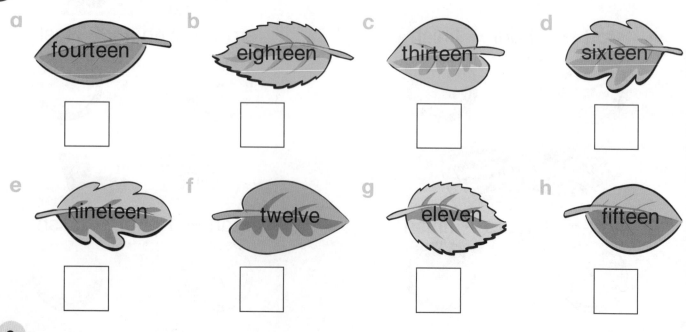

a fourteen   b eighteen   c thirteen   d sixteen

e nineteen   f twelve   g eleven   h fifteen

Patterns and sequences

Colours, **shapes** and **lines** can make different patterns and sequences.

1 Continue drawing each pattern.

a

b

c

d

2 Draw over these. Colour to make a pattern.

a

b

Missing numbers

Learn the order of numbers to **20**.

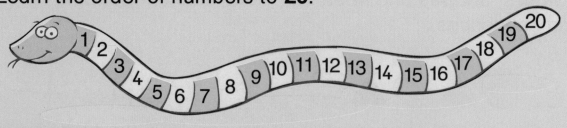

Count backwards and forwards along the snake.

1 Write the missing numbers.

a 7 8 __ __ 11 __ __ 14 __ __

b __ __ __ __ 15 16 17 __ __ 20

c 18 17 16 __ __ 13 __ __ __ __

d __ __ 10 9 __ __ __ 5 4 __

2 Write these numbers as words. What is the hidden, shaded number?

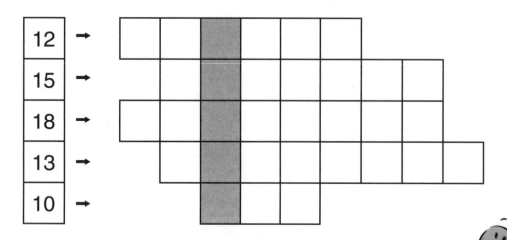

12	➡
15	➡
18	➡
13	➡
10	➡

The shaded number is ☐.

Counting forwards and backwards

Practise counting **forwards** and **backwards** on a number line.

Follow the jumps with your finger.

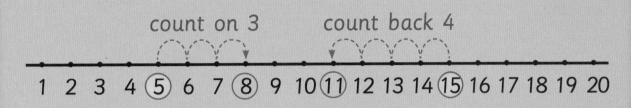

count on 3   count back 4

1 2 3 4 ⑤ 6 7 ⑧ 9 10 ⑪ 12 13 14 ⑮ 16 17 18 19 20

1 Write the answers. Use the number line above to help.

a 3 → Count on 2 → ☐   e ☐ ← Count back 2 ← 8

b 7 → Count on 3 → ☐   f ☐ ← Count back 4 ← 12

c 11 → Count on 5 → ☐   g ☐ ← Count back 3 ← 16

d 10 → Count on 4 → ☐   h ☐ ← Count back 5 ← 14

2 Draw the jumps to show the counting on or back. Circle the number you finish on.

a Count on 4

c Count back 2

b Count on 3

d Count back 5

Starting to add

We use the **+** sign to show **adding**.

= is the **equals** sign.

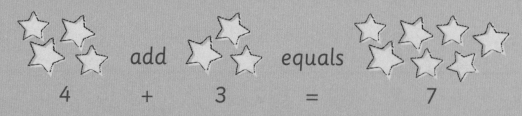

| 4 | + | 3 | = | 7 |

1 Write the numbers for these additions.

a

☐ + ☐ = ☐

c

☐ + ☐ = ☐

b

☐ + ☐ = ☐

d

☐ + ☐ = ☐

2 Draw some more spots to help work out the missing numbers.

a

3 + ☐ = 7

c

4 + ☐ = 6

b

2 + ☐ = 5

d

5 + ☐ = 9

3-D shapes

Look around you for these 3-D shapes. Try to remember their names.

cuboid   cube   sphere   cone   cylinder

1 Draw lines to join each shape to its name.

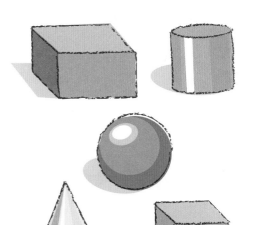

cone

cube

cylinder

cuboid

sphere

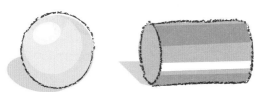

2 Colour in the shapes that have all flat faces.

a
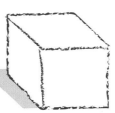

b

c

d

e
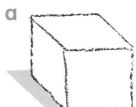

f
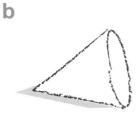

g
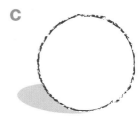

h
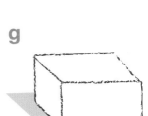

Starting to take away

We use the – sign when we **subtract** or **take away**.

$$5 - 2 = 3$$

start with 5   take away 2   3 left

1 Cross out some buns to help answer these.

a

$$5 - 4 = \boxed{}$$

c

$$4 - 2 = \boxed{}$$

b

$$6 - 2 = \boxed{}$$

d

$$6 - 3 = \boxed{}$$

2 Write out a subtraction for each of these.

a

$$\boxed{} - \boxed{} = \boxed{}$$

c

$$\boxed{} - \boxed{} = \boxed{}$$

b

$$\boxed{} - \boxed{} = \boxed{}$$

d

$$\boxed{} - \boxed{} = \boxed{}$$

Recognising coins

Try to learn these **coins**.

p means pence.
There are 50 pence
or pennies in 50p.

| 1p | 2p | 5p | 10p | 20p | 50p |

1 Cross out the odd one in each set.

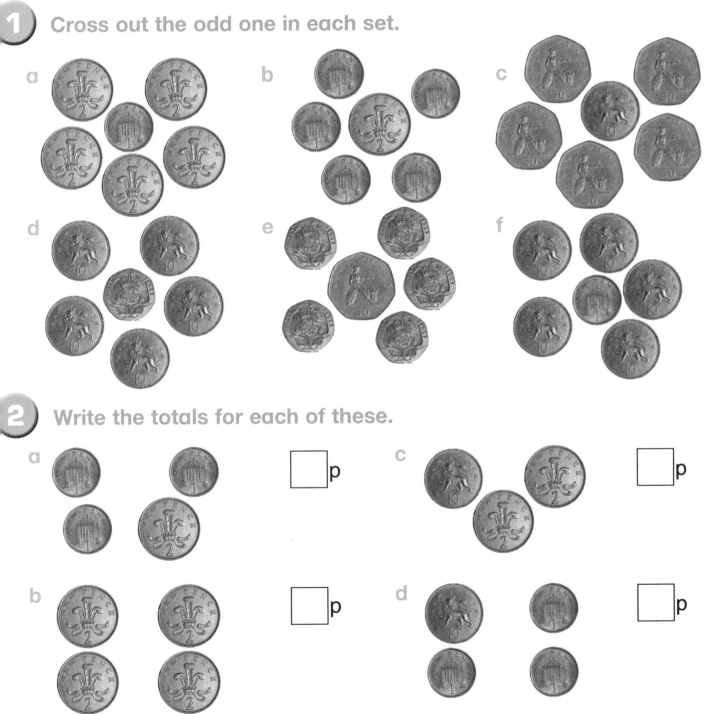

a

b

c

d

e

f

2 Write the totals for each of these.

a [ ]p

c [ ]p

b [ ]p

d [ ]p

More or less

Look at the way numbers change if you make them **1** or **10** more or less.

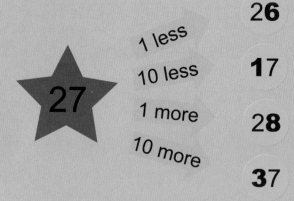

1 less	26
10 less	17
1 more	28
10 more	37

1 Answer these.

a Add 1 more.

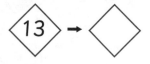

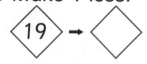

c Add 10 more.

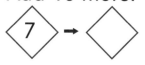

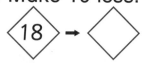

b Make 1 less.

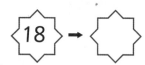

d Make 10 less.

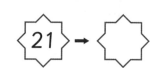

2 Count how much money is in each purse.

a Add 1p and write the total amount.

b Add 10p and write the total amount.

p p p p

Odds and evens

Say these odd and even numbers out loud.

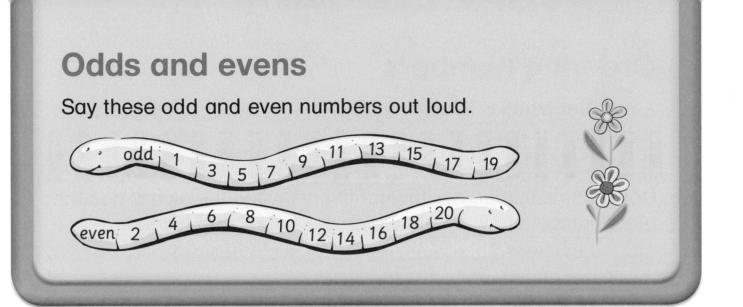

1. **Try to do these odd and even problems.**

a Tick the shields with an even number of dots.

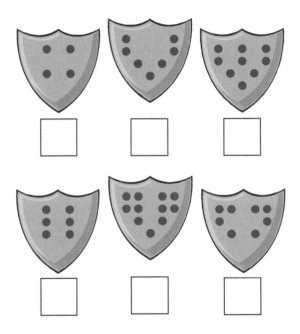

b Colour all the badges with even numbers.

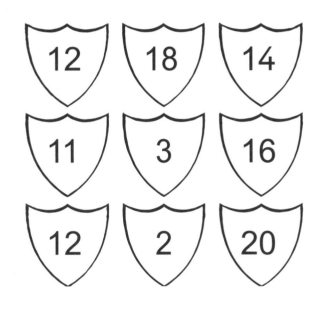

2. **Now try these problems.**

a Write the next odd numbers.

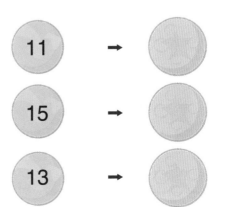

11 →

15 →

13 →

b Write the next even numbers.

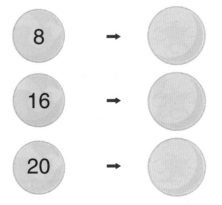

8 →

16 →

20 →

Ordering numbers

A **number track** will help you to learn the order of numbers.

Cover some numbers with your fingers without looking. Use the other numbers to work out which ones you have hidden.

1 These numbers have fallen off the washing on each line. Put them back in the correct order.

a
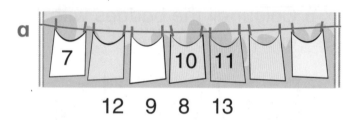

12   9   8   13

c
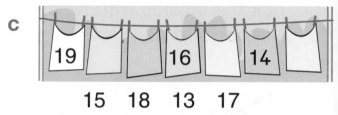

15   18   13   17

b
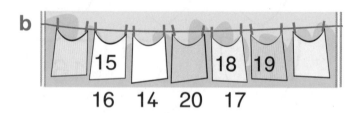

16   14   20   17

d
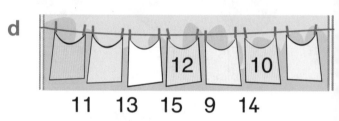

11   13   15   9   14

2 Draw lines to join the price labels to the correct tins. The prices should be in order.

Lowest ⟶ Highest

Teen numbers

Teen numbers are made from a **10** and some **1s**.

Read these numbers aloud.

13	14	15	16	17	18	19
10+3	10+4	10+5	10+6	10+7	10+8	10+9

11 and 12 are also made from a 10 and 1s but do not end in *-teen*.

1 Write the missing numbers to show 10s and 1s.

a fifteen ➡ [10] + [ ]   f twelve ➡ [ ] + [ ]

b eighteen ➡ [ ] + [ ]   g fourteen ➡ [ ] + [ ]

c eleven ➡ [ ] + [ ]   h thirteen ➡ [ ] + [ ]

d sixteen ➡ [ ] + [ ]   i seventeen ➡ [ ] + [ ]

e nineteen ➡ [ ] + [ ]

2 Write these answers in words.

a 10 + 3 ➡   e 10 + 2 ➡

b 10 + 1 ➡   f 10 + 6 ➡

c 10 + 9 ➡   g 10 + 7 ➡

d 10 + 4 ➡   h 10 + 8 ➡

Halves and quarters

A half shows one of two equal parts.

This arrow is pointing to half a cake.

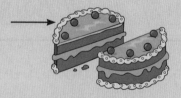

Half of these candles are red.

A quarter is one of four equal parts.

This arrow is pointing to a quarter of a sandwich.

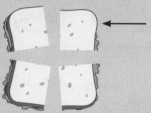

A quarter of these balloons are round.

1 Look at these shapes.

a Colour half of each plate.

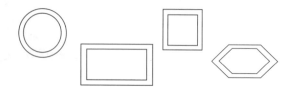

b Colour a quarter of this bar.

2 Look at these groups.

a Draw a loop around half of these stars.

b Draw a loop around a quarter of these moons.

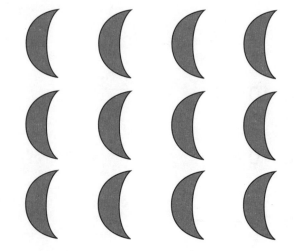

Ordinal numbers

1st, 2nd, 3rd... are called ordinal numbers.

They show the **order of things**.

first	second	third	fourth	fifth	sixth	seventh	eighth
1st	2nd	3rd	4th	5th	6th	7th	8th

1 **Look at the order of the letters in the alphabet.**

A B C D E F G H I J K L M N O P Q R S T U V W X Y Z

Complete these.

The 1st letter is ☐.   F is the ☐ letter.

The 5th letter is ☐.   C is the ☐ letter.

The 7th letter is ☐.   L is the ☐ letter.

The 4th letter is ☐.   P is the ☐ letter.

The last letter is ☐.   B is the ☐ letter.

2 **Use the alphabet order to work out these word puzzles.**

a 13th   1st   20th   8th   19th

[M] ☐ ☐ ☐ ☐

b 13th   1st   7th   9th   3rd

[M] ☐ ☐ ☐ ☐

Now try making up your own puzzles.

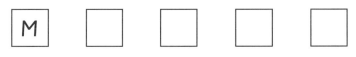

Days of the week

Try to learn the **order** of the days of the week.

1 **How well have you learnt the days of the week?**

a Draw lines to join each day to the one that follows it.

b Now join each day to the one that comes before it.

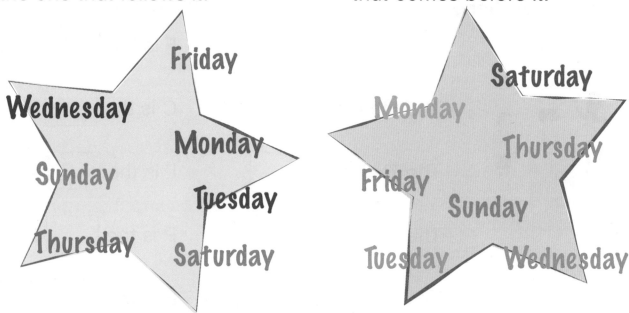

2 **Fill in the gaps to show what day it is.**

W e __ __ __ __ d a y

S __ __ u r __ __ y

F __ __ __ a y

__ o n d __ __

S u __ __ a y

__ __ u r s d __ __

T __ e __ d __ y

MONDAY
TUESDAY
WEDNESDAY
THURSDAY
FRIDAY
SATURDAY
SUNDAY

Money

You need to know what these **coins** are worth.

1p 2p 5p 10p 20p 50p

p means pence. There are 50 pence or pennies in 50p.

1 Add up the value of these coins to find the total.

a  p

c  p

b  p

d  p

2 Draw the coins you would use to buy these sweets.

a
7p

b
16p

c
11p

Adding

Use a **number track** like this to help you add.

$$2 + 3 = 5$$
+3

0 1 2 3 4 5 6 7 8 9 10

1 Use the number track to help you add these.

a 3 + 4 = ☐

b 1 + 3 = ☐

c 4 + 2 = ☐

d 0 + 2 = ☐

e 3 + 3 = ☐

f 2 + 5 = ☐

g 4 + 4 = ☐

h 3 + 2 = ☐

i 0 + 5 = ☐

j 5 + 3 = ☐

k 4 + 5 = ☐

l 6 + 3 = ☐

m 5 + 1 = ☐

n 8 + 2 = ☐

o 3 + 7 = ☐

2 Write the numbers coming out of the machines.

a 3 ☐

b 5 ☐

c 2 ☐

d 6 ☐

e 2 ☐

f 5 ☐

g 4 ☐

h 1 ☐

Taking away

You can count back along a number line to help you **subtract** or **take away**.

$$8 - 3 = 5$$

1 Use the number lines to help you complete these.

a 5 6 7 8 9 10

$9 - 4 = \boxed{}$

b 1 2 3 4 5 6 7

$7 - \boxed{} = 3$

c 2 3 4 5 6 7 8

$8 - \boxed{} = 4$

d 5 6 7 8 9 10

$10 - \boxed{} = 7$

e 2 3 4 5 6 7 8 9

$8 - 5 = \boxed{}$

f 1 2 3 4 5 6 7

$5 - \boxed{} = 3$

2 Colour the tyre which gives a different answer to the others in the pile.

a

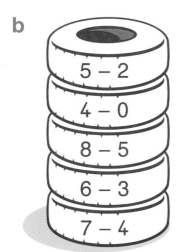

$8 - 3$

$10 - 5$

$9 - 4$

$6 - 1$

$5 - 2$

b

$5 - 2$

$4 - 0$

$8 - 5$

$6 - 3$

$7 - 4$

c

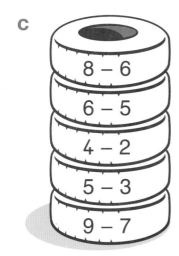

$8 - 6$

$6 - 5$

$4 - 2$

$5 - 3$

$9 - 7$

25

Measuring

Mass and capacity are 2 ways of measuring.

Mass

We use the words *heavy* and *light* when talking about mass, or weight.

Capacity

The capacity is how much something holds.

1 Which objects are heavy and which are light? Circle the lightest ones.

a

b

c

2 Look at these containers. Draw lines to join them in order. Start with the smallest capacity.

Counting patterns

Use this number grid to help you with **counting patterns**.

71	72	73	74	75	76	77	78	79	80
81	82	83	84	85	86	87	88	89	90
91	92	93	94	95	96	97	98	99	100
101	102	103	104	105	106	107	108	109	110

1 **Look at the numbers on the track.**

Colour the number 72 red.

Miss out number 73 and colour number 74 red.

Miss out number 75 and colour number 76 red.

Continue colouring this pattern.

71	72	73	74	75	76	77	78	79	80	81	82	83	84	85	86	87	88	89	90

a The red numbers are called _____ numbers.

b The other numbers are called _____ numbers.

2 **Continue these counting patterns.**

a 110 109 108 107

b 84 86 88 90

c 89 91 93 95

d 75 80 85 90

e 110 108 106 104

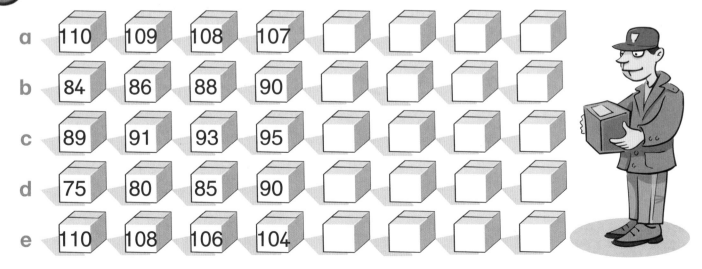

Half past time

When the **minute hand** points to the **6** it shows a half past time.

The hour hand is past the 7.

This clock shows half past 7, or 7:30.

1 Write out these times in the boxes.

a

half past ☐

c

half past ☐

e

half past ☐

b

half past ☐

d

half past ☐

f

half past ☐

2 Draw lines to join the clocks that show the same time.

a

b

c

Using doubles

Use **doubles** to help you with other additions.

Double 3 is 6.

    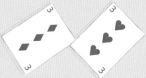

$3 + 3 = 6$ so $3 + 4 = 7$

---

1 Write the answers in the boxes.

a  $3 + 3 = \boxed{}$ so  $3 + 4 = \boxed{}$

b $4 + 4 = \boxed{}$ so  $4 + 5 = \boxed{}$

c $5 + 5 = \boxed{}$ so  $5 + 6 = \boxed{}$

d $6 + 6 = \boxed{}$ so  $6 + 7 = \boxed{}$

e $7 + 7 = \boxed{}$ so  $7 + 8 = \boxed{}$

---

2 Draw more dots on each domino to match the total in the box below.

a  b  c  d  e

| 9 | 7 | 5 | 11 | 12 |

Totalling 20

Try to learn the **pairs of numbers** that total 20.

$$13 \quad 15 \quad 12 \quad 9$$
$$7 \quad 5 \quad 8 \quad 11$$

Use the totals for 10 to help you.
$8 + 2 = 10$ so $8 + 12$ is 10 more.

1 **Write the missing numbers.**

a $3 + \boxed{} = 20$ e $\boxed{} + 0 = 20$ i $1 + \boxed{} = 20$

b $8 + \boxed{} = 20$ f $\boxed{} + 19 = 20$ j $\boxed{} + 4 = 20$

c $14 + \boxed{} = 20$ g $\boxed{} + 8 = 20$ k $10 + \boxed{} = 20$

d $5 + \boxed{} = 20$ h $\boxed{} + 17 = 20$ l $\boxed{} + 15 = 20$

2 **Corner numbers add up to 20. Write the missing corner numbers for each of these.**

a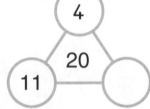

c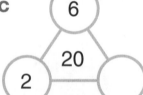

e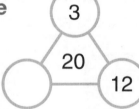

b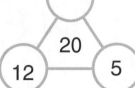

d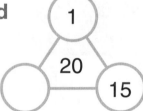

Finding the difference

A **number track** is very useful for finding the difference between 2 numbers.

Count on from 4 to 7, counting the jumps.

The difference between 4 and 7 is 3.

1 Draw the jumps to find the difference between these pairs of numbers in red.

a

The difference is ☐.

c

The difference is ☐.

b

The difference is ☐.

d

The difference is ☐.

2 Draw lines to join the pairs of numbers with a difference of 4.

Test 1 Counting to 10

Use these **numbers** to help you.

0 zero	1 one	2 two	3 three	4 four	5 five
	•	• •	•• •	•• ••	••• ••

6 six	7 seven	8 eight	9 nine	10 ten
••• •••	•••• •••	•••• ••••	••••• ••••	••••• •••••

Count the marbles. Write the total in the box.

1.

2.

3.

4.

5.

6.

7.

8.

9.

10.

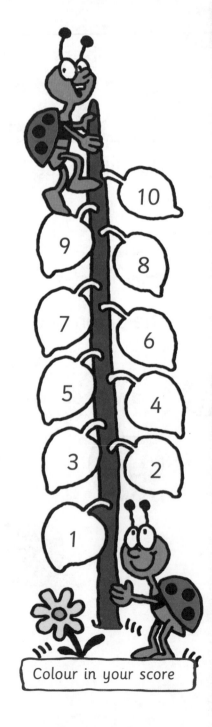

10
9
8
7
6
5
4
3
2
1

Colour in your score

32

Test 2 Reading and writing numbers to 20

Use these **numbers** and **words** to help you.

0 zero	**1** one	**2** two	**3** three	**4** four	**5** five
6 six	**7** seven	**8** eight	**9** nine	**10** ten	
11 eleven	**12** twelve	**13** thirteen	**14** fourteen	**15** fifteen	
16 sixteen	**17** seventeen	**18** eighteen	**19** nineteen	**20** twenty	

Write the number.

1. six

2. eight

3. twelve

4. fifteen

5. twenty

Write the word.

6. 3

7. 9

8. 11

9. 17

10. 19

Colour in your score

Test 3 Addition to 10

Number lines help you to **add**.

4 + 3 = 7

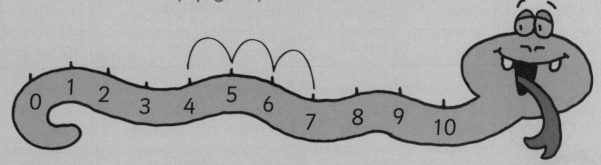

Write the answers to these sums.

1.   6 + 3 =

2.   2 + 5 =

3.   7 + 2 =

4.   4 + 4 =

5.   5 + 4 =

6.   1 + 7 =

7.   5 + 3 =

8.   6 + 4 =

9.   3 + 7 =

10. 8 + 1 =

Colour in your score

34

Test 4 Measures: length

shortest   tallest

Tick the shortest.

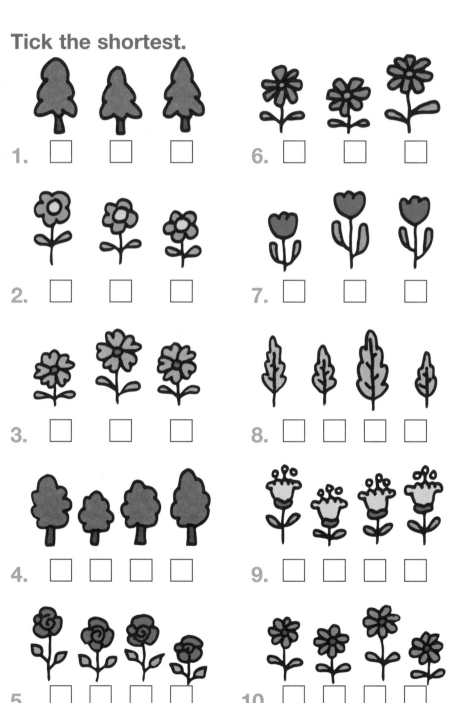

1.

2.

3.

4.

5.

6.

7.

8.

9.

10.

10
9
8
7
6
5
4
3
2
1

Colour in your score

35

Test 5 **2-D shapes**

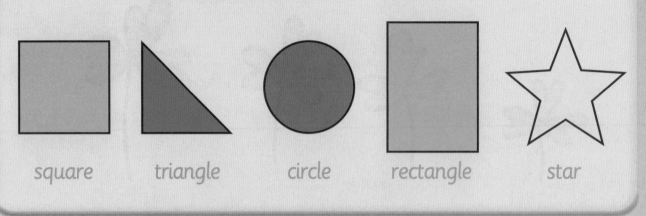

square   triangle   circle   rectangle   star

Name each shape.   **Finish drawing each shape.**

1. _____

2. _____

3. _____

4. _____

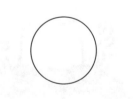

5. _____

6.   rectangle

7.   triangle

8.   square

9.   star

10.   circle

Colour in your score

Test 6 Counting sequences to 12

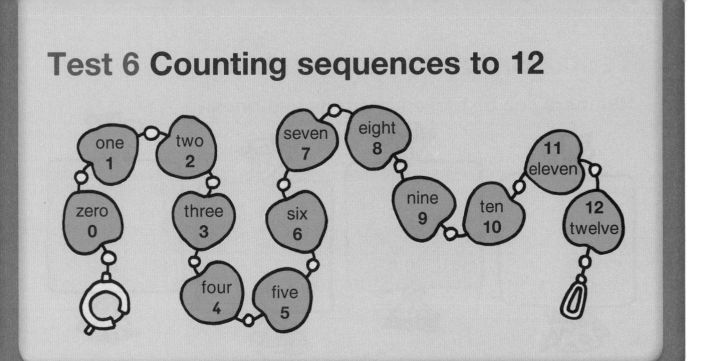

Write the missing numbers.

1. | 2 | 3 | 4 | | |

6. | | | 10 | 11 | 12 |

2. | | | 7 | 8 | 9 |

7. | | 4 | 5 | | |

3. | | | 9 | 10 | |

8. | 12 | 11 | 10 | | |

4. | 9 | 8 | 7 | | |

9. | | | 6 | 5 | 4 |

5. | | | 4 | 3 | |

10. | | | 8 | 7 | |

Colour in your score

Test 7 Breaking up numbers

Numbers can be broken into **tens** and **ones**.

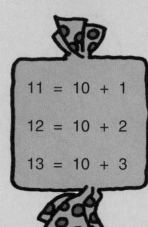

11 = 10 + 1

12 = 10 + 2

13 = 10 + 3

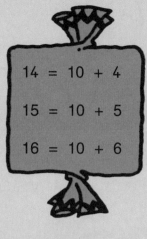

14 = 10 + 4

15 = 10 + 5

16 = 10 + 6

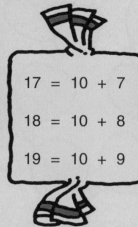

17 = 10 + 7

18 = 10 + 8

19 = 10 + 9

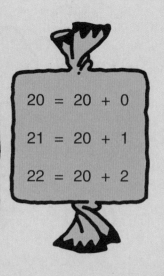

20 = 20 + 0

21 = 20 + 1

22 = 20 + 2

Fill in the missing numbers.

1.   16 = 10 + ☐

2.   14 = 10 + ☐

3.   17 = 10 + ☐

4.   18 = 10 + ☐

5.   21 = 20 + ☐

6.   17 = ☐ + 7

7.   13 = ☐ + 3

8.   12 = ☐ + 2

9.   19 = ☐ + 9

10. 11 = ☐ + 1

Colour in your score

Test 8 Adding and subtracting to 20

When **adding**, you can **count on** from the **larger number**.

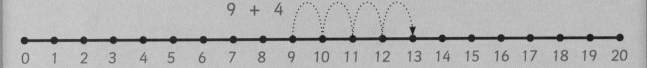

$$9 + 4$$

| 0 | 1 | 2 | 3 | 4 | 5 | 6 | 7 | 8 | 9 | 10 | 11 | 12 | 13 | 14 | 15 | 16 | 17 | 18 | 19 | 20 |

When **subtracting**, you can **count back** from the **larger number**.

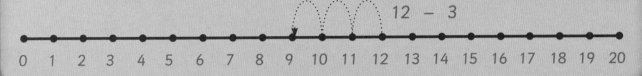

$$12 - 3$$

| 0 | 1 | 2 | 3 | 4 | 5 | 6 | 7 | 8 | 9 | 10 | 11 | 12 | 13 | 14 | 15 | 16 | 17 | 18 | 19 | 20 |

Write the answers.

1. $8 + 5 =$ ☐

2. $2 + 13 =$ ☐

3. $11 + 4 =$ ☐

4. $3 + 17 =$ ☐

5. $15 + 4 =$ ☐

6. $16 - 3 =$ ☐

7. $20 - 2 =$ ☐

8. $18 - 5 =$ ☐

9. $11 - 2 =$ ☐

10. $15 - 4 =$ ☐

Colour in your score

10
9
8
7
6
5
4
3
2
1

Test 9 Time: o'clock

The **minute hand** points to **12** for **o'clock times**.

8 o'clock

Hands on a clock move clockwise.

Write the times.

Draw the missing hand.

1.  ☐ o'clock

2.  ☐ o'clock

3.  ☐ o'clock

4.  ☐ o'clock

5.  ☐ o'clock

6.

six o'clock

7.

four o'clock

8.

eight o'clock

9.

seven o'clock

10.

two o'clock

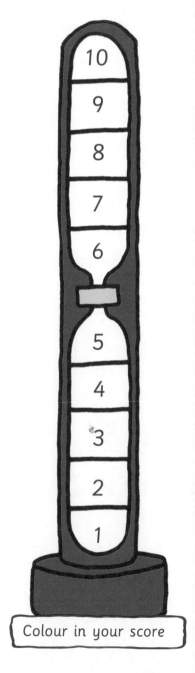

Colour in your score

40

Test 10 Data diagrams

Some diagrams show **opposites**.

square	not square
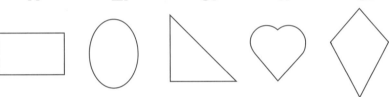	

Draw each shape on the diagram.

1.	2.	3.	4.	5.

straight sides	not straight sides

Write each number on the diagram.

6. 3   7. 11   8. 15   9. 8   10. 10

less than 10	not less than 10

10
9
8
7
6
5
4
3
2
1

Colour in your score

41

Test 11 Counting sequences to 20

Say these numbers **forwards** and **backwards**.

Write the missing numbers.

1.  8 9 10

2.  10 11 12

3.  15 16 17

4.  15 14 13

5. 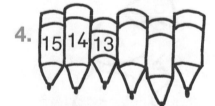 10 9 8

6.  14 15 16

7.  8 9 10

8.  20 19 18

9.  16 15 14

10.  19 17 15

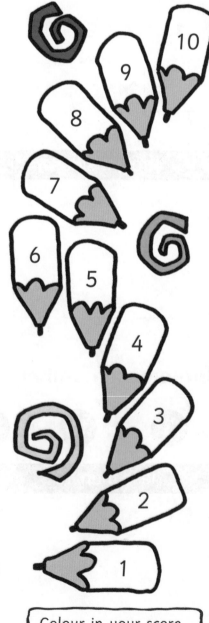

Colour in your score

42

Test 12 **Ordinal numbers**

Some numbers show the **order** of things.

1. Colour the 3rd snail.

2. Colour the 1st star.

3. Colour the 4th spider.

4. Colour the 2nd ladybird.

5. Colour the last worm.

6. Colour the 3rd letter.

PETER

7. Colour the 4th letter.

PAUL

8. Colour the 5th letter.

SALLY

9. Colour the 2nd letter.

HARRY

10. Colour the last letter.

GITA

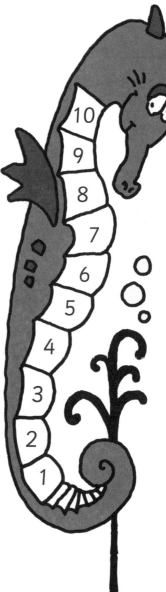

Colour in your score

Test 13 Subtraction within 10

Jumping **back** is the same as **subtraction**.

start

$$10 - 4 = 6$$

Use the number line to help answer these.

1. 7 − 2 =

2. 8 − 4 =

3. 5 − 5 =

4. 9 − 1 =

5. 8 − 6 =

6. 7 − 5 =

7. 10 − 8 =

8. 6 − 4 =

9. 10 − 5 =

10. 9 − 3 =

Colour in your score

10
9
8
7
6
5
4
3
2
1

Test 14 Measures: weight

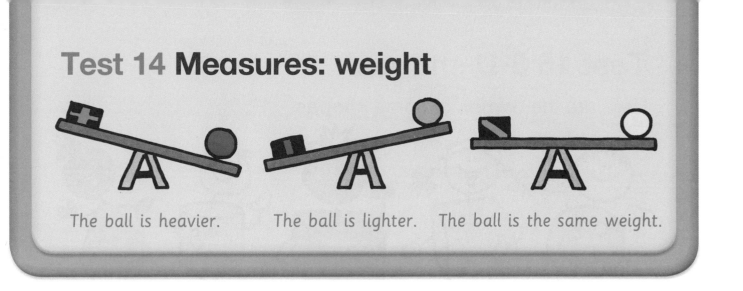

The ball is heavier.   The ball is lighter.   The ball is the same weight.

Underline the word to show whether the ball is heavier, lighter or the same weight.

1. heavier lighter same

2. heavier lighter same

3. heavier lighter same

4. heavier lighter same

5. heavier lighter same

6. heavier lighter same

7. heavier lighter same

8. heavier lighter same

9. heavier lighter same

10. heavier lighter same

10
9
8
7
6
5
4
3
2
1

Colour in your score

Test 15 3-D shapes

Here are the **names** of some **shapes**.

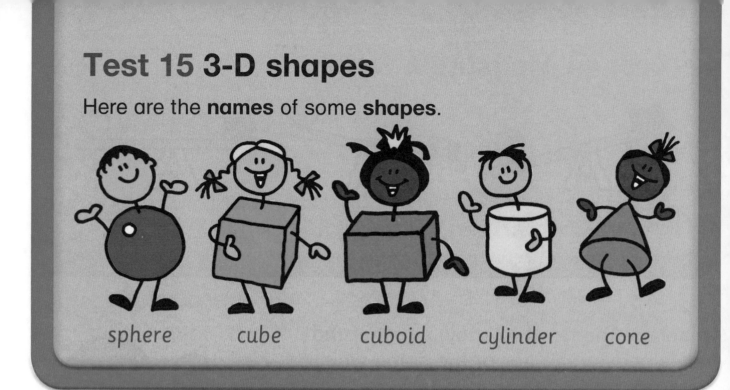

sphere   cube   cuboid   cylinder   cone

Join each shape to its name.

1.  | sphere | 6.

2.  | cone | 7.

3. | cuboid | 8.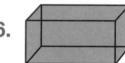

4. | cylinder | 9.

5. 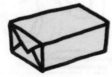 | cube | 10.

Colour in your score

10 9 8 7 6 5 4 3 2 1

Test 16 Counting on and back

It is very useful to be able to **count on** and **back**.

count on 3   count back 3

Write these missing numbers.

1. 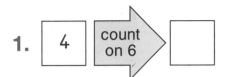 4 | count on 6 | ☐

6. count on
   ⃝ 7 ☐ ⃝ 12

2. 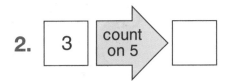 3 | count on 5 | ☐

7. count on
   ⃝ 9 ☐ ⃝ 15

3. 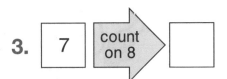 7 | count on 8 | ☐

8. count back
   ⃝ 12 ☐ ⃝ 8

4. 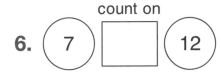 12 | count back 2 | ☐

9. count back
   ⃝ 13 ☐ ⃝ 6

5. 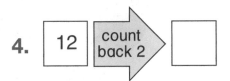 17 | count back 5 | ☐

10. count back
    ⃝ 20 ☐ ⃝ 13

Colour in your score

Test 17 Comparing numbers

13 is bigger than **9**   **6** is smaller than **12**

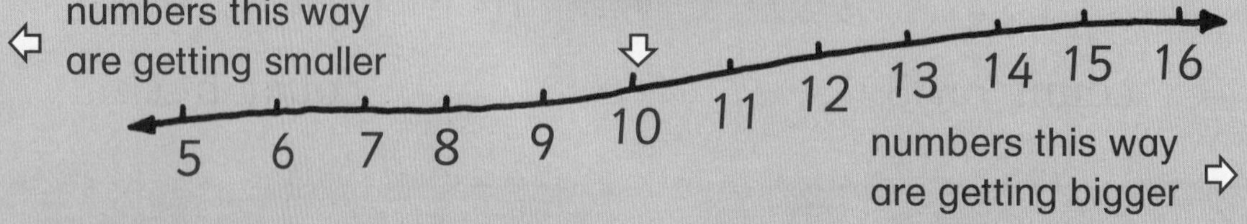

numbers this way
are getting smaller

5   6   7   8   9   10   11   12   13   14   15   16

numbers this way
are getting bigger

Colour the bigger number.   **Colour the smaller number.**

1. 12   7

6. 4   7

2. 11   14

7. 11   19

3. 15   12

8. 13   12

4. 10   11

9. 15   8

5. 13   16

10. 13   17

10
9
8
7
6
5
4
3
2
1

Colour in your score

Test 18 Addition using doubles

Near doubles can help us add.

 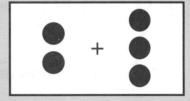

2 + 2 = 4   2 + 3 = 5

Add these doubles.

1. • • = ☐

2. 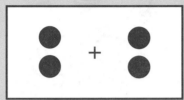 = ☐

3. = ☐

4. = ☐

5. = ☐

Add these near doubles.

6. | 4 | 3 | = ☐

7. | 5 | 6 | = ☐

8. | 4 | 5 | = ☐

9. | 6 | 7 | = ☐

10. | 7 | 8 | = ☐

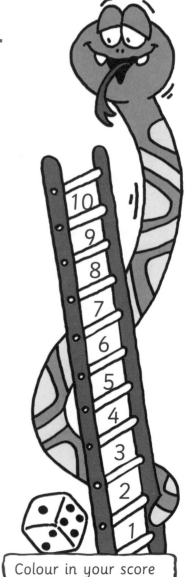

Colour in your score

49

Test 19 Time: half past

The **minute hand** points to **6** for **half past** times.

half past 8

Write the times.

1.  half past [ ]

2. half past [ ]

3.  half past [ ]

4.  half past [ ]

5.  half past [ ]

Draw the missing hand.

6.  half past 1

7.  half past 11

8.  half past 4

9.  half past 2

10.  half past 9

Colour in your score

50

Test 20 Data graphs

This **graph** shows children's favourite ice-creams.

vanilla	🍦	🍦	🍦	🍦	🍦	🍦
mint	🍦	🍦	🍦	🍦		
lemon	🍦					
chocolate	🍦	🍦	🍦	🍦	🍦	
orange	🍦	🍦	🍦			

How many children's favourite was:

1. chocolate?

2. mint?

3. vanilla?

4. orange?

5. lemon?

6. Which was the favourite?

7. Which was the least favourite?

8. Which was chosen by 4 children?

9. Which was chosen by 3 children?

10. How many children were there altogether?

Colour in your score

Test 21 Counting in steps

A **number grid** helps you to see **number patterns**.

61	62	63	64	65	66	67	68	69	70
71	72	73	74	75	76	77	78	79	80
81	82	83	84	85	86	87	88	89	90
91	92	93	94	95	96	97	98	99	100
101	102	103	104	105	106	107	108	109	110

Count in 2s to complete the pattern.

1. | 64 | 66 | 68 | | | |

2. | 110 | 108 | 106 | | | |

3. | 93 | 95 | 97 | | | |

4. | 75 | 77 | 79 | | | |

5. | 101 | 99 | 97 | | | |

Count in 5s to complete the pattern.

6. | 65 | 70 | 75 | | | |

7. | 110 | 105 | 100 | | | |

8. | 90 | 85 | 80 | | | |

9. | 75 | 80 | 85 | | | |

10. | 85 | 90 | 95 | | | |

10
9
8
7
6
5
4
3
2
1

Colour in your score

52

Test 22 Halves and quarters

Half of these apples are red.

A quarter of these bananas are in a box.

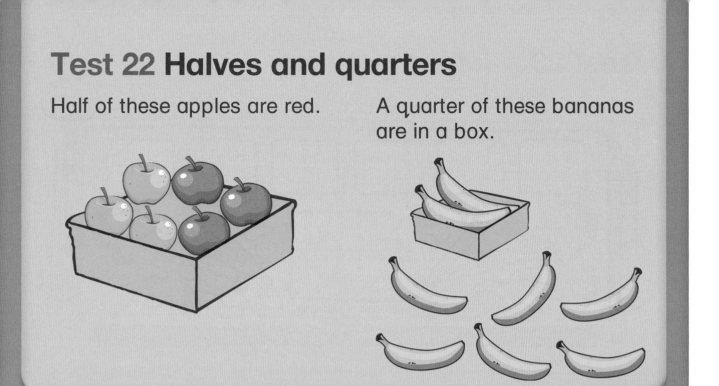

Colour half.

1.

2.

3.

4.

5.

Draw a loop around a quarter.

6.

7.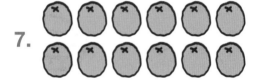

8.

9.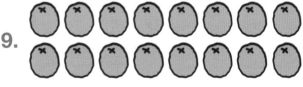

10.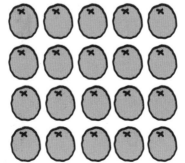

Colour in your score

53

Test 23 Addition patterns

Addition facts to **10** are important.

| 10 + 0 | 9 + 1 | 8 + 2 | 7 + 3 | 6 + 4 | 5 + 5 |
| 0 + 10 | 1 + 9 | 2 + 8 | 3 + 7 | 4 + 6 | |

10

Write the missing number in the box.

1. 7 + ☐ = 10

2. 4 + ☐ = 10

3. 8 + ☐ = 10

4. 3 + ☐ = 10

5. 9 + ☐ = 10

6. ☐ + 1 = 10

7. ☐ + 4 = 10

8. ☐ + 6 = 10

9. ☐ + 8 = 10

10. ☐ + 3 = 10

Colour in your score

54

Test 24 Measures: capacity

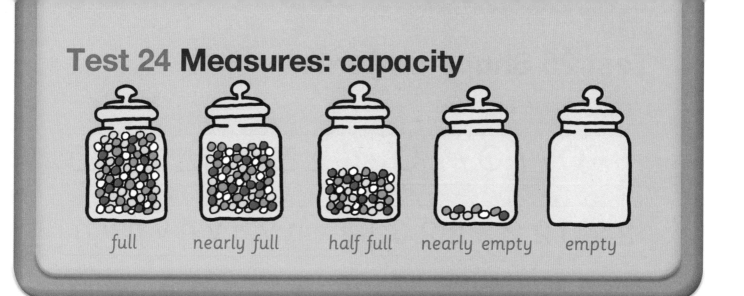

full   nearly full   half full   nearly empty   empty

Colour the mugs and bowls to show how full they are.

1. half full

2. empty

3. nearly full

4. nearly empty

5. full

6. full

7. nearly empty

8. empty

9. nearly full

10. half full

Colour in your score

10
9
8
7
6
5
4
3
2
1

Test 25 Shape patterns

Look at these **patterns**.

/ / O / / O / / O	△ □ △ □ △ □ △ □
2 2 3 2 2 3 2 2 3	v n v n v n v n v n

Continue each pattern.

1.

2.

3.

4.

5.

6. 1 1 2 1 1 2

7.

8.

9. △ □ ◦ △ □ ◦

10. 1 2 3 1 2 3

10
9
8
7
6
5
4
3
2
1

Colour in your score

Test 26 Odds and evens

even numbers				
2	4	6	8	10
These end in 2, 4, 6, 8, or 0.				

odd numbers				
1	3	5	7	9
These end in 1, 3, 5, 7, or 9.				

Write the next odd number.

1. (3) ( )

2. (7) ( )

3. (11)  ( )

4. (15) ( )

5. (19) ( )

Write the next even number.

6. [4] [ ]

7. [8] [ ]

8. [12] [ ]

9. [16] [ ]

10. [20] [ ]

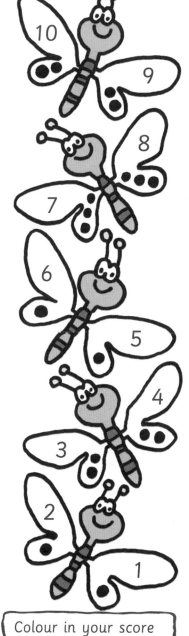

Colour in your score

Test 27 Ordering numbers

Number tracks help us to put numbers in **order**.

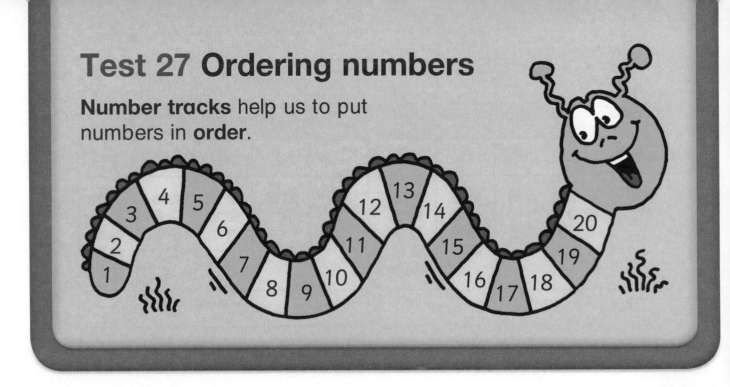

Write these numbers in order.

1. | 8 | 1 | 4 | 2 | 6 | ➡ | 1 | | | | |

2. | 3 | 4 | 7 | 9 | 2 | ➡ | 2 | | | | |

3. | 10 | 2 | 9 | 6 | 4 | ➡ | 2 | | | | |

4. | 10 | 3 | 15 | 5 | 7 | ➡ | 3 | | | | |

5. | 5 | 11 | 8 | 17 | 9 | ➡ | 5 | | | | |

6. | 15 | 10 | 17 | 9 | 20 | ➡ | 9 | | | | |

7. | 11 | 19 | 10 | 14 | 12 | ➡ | 10 | | | | |

8. | 11 | 17 | 13 | 12 | 19 | ➡ | 11 | | | | |

9. | 14 | 16 | 13 | 20 | 15 | ➡ | 13 | | | | |

10. | 17 | 16 | 20 | 18 | 19 | ➡ | 16 | | | | |

Colour in your score

Test 28 Adding and subtracting

A **number line** will help with **adding** and **subtracting**.

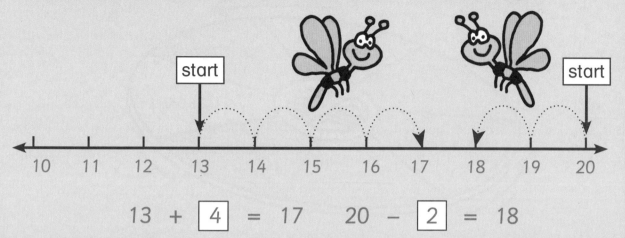

$$13 + \boxed{4} = 17 \qquad 20 - \boxed{2} = 18$$

Write the missing number in the box.

1. $13 + \boxed{} = 20$

2. $12 + \boxed{} = 17$

3. $17 + \boxed{} = 20$

4. $14 + \boxed{} = 18$

5. $13 + \boxed{} = 19$

6. $18 - \boxed{} = 14$

7. $17 - \boxed{} = 11$

8. $15 - \boxed{} = 12$

9. $19 - \boxed{} = 16$

10. $14 - \boxed{} = 10$

Colour in your score

Test 29 Days of the week

Learn the **order** of the **days**.

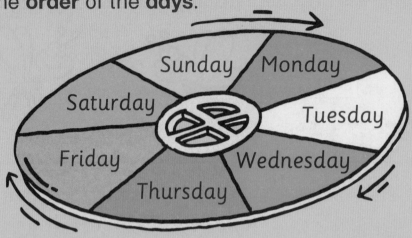

Write the day before:

1. Monday

2. Thursday

3. Wednesday

4. Tuesday

5. Saturday

Write the day after:

6. Friday

7. Sunday

8. Tuesday

9. Saturday

10. Wednesday

Colour in your score

Test 30 Learning to tally

Tally marks show how **many**.

1	2	3	4	5
I	II	III	IIII	IHI
6	**7**	**8**	**9**	**10**
IHI I	IHI II	IHI III	IHI IIII	IHI IHI

Make tally marks to show how many fish and insects there are.

1.		
2.		
3.		
4.		
5.		

6.		
7.		
8.		
9.		
10.		

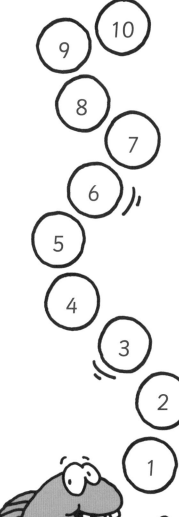

Colour in your score

61

ANSWERS

Page 2

1

2 one → 1   six → 6
two → 2   seven → 7
three → 3   eight → 8
four → 4   nine → 9
five → 5   ten → 10

Page 3

1 a 8   **b** 6   **c** 9
  d 11   **e** 14   **f** 15

2 There are 20 fish altogether.

Page 4

1 a 3 and 2 makes a total of 5
  b 5 and 3 makes a total of 8
  c 4 and 3 makes a total of 7

2 Check there are now 8 beans in each set.

Page 5

1

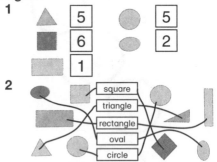

2

Page 6

1 a

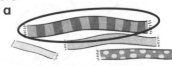

b

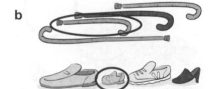

2 a 3 pennies
  b 5 pennies
  c 2 pennies
  d 4 pennies
  e 3 pennies

Page 7

1 a 7 o'clock
  b 1 o'clock

c 6 o'clock
d 8 o'clock
e 9 o'clock
f 3 o'clock
g 11 o'clock
h 10 o'clock

2 a  **c**

b   **d**

Page 8

1 Check child's writing.

2 a 14   **b** 18   **c** 13
  d 16   **e** 19   **f** 12
  g 11   **h** 15

Page 9

1 Check child's patterns.

2 Check child's patterns.

Page 10

The missing numbers are in **bold**.

1 a 7, 8, **9**, **10**, 11, **12**, **13**, 14, **15**, **16**

  b **11**, **12**, **13**, **14**, 15, 16, 17, **18**, **19**, 20

  c 18, 17, 16, **15**, **14**, 13, **12**, **11**, **10**, **9**

  d **12**, **11**, 10, 9, **8**, **7**, **6**, 5, 4, **3**

2

t	w	e	l	v	e	
		f	i	f	t	e	e	n
e	i	g	h	t	e	e	n
	t	h	i	r	t	e	e	n
		t	e	n

The shaded number is 8.

Page 11

1 a 5   **d** 14   **g** 13
  b 10   **e** 6   **h** 9
  c 16   **f** 8

2 a 3 4 5 6 ⑦ 8 9
  b 5 6 7 8 ⑨ 10 11
  c 2 3 4 ⑤ 6 7 8
  d 6 ⑦ 8 9 10 11 12

Page 12

1 a 3 + 2 = 5   **c** 4 + 4 = 8
  b 3 + 3 = 6   **d** 5 + 3 = 8

2 a 4   **c** 2
  b 3   **d** 4

Page 13

1

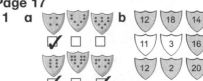

2 Check child has coloured a, g and h.

Page 14

1 Check child has crossed out correct number of buns.
  a 1   **c** 2
  b 4   **d** 3

2 a 6 − 4 = 2   **c** 5 − 3 = 2
  b 7 − 3 = 4   **d** 6 − 5 = 1

Page 15

1 Check these coins have been crossed out.
  a 1p   **d** 20p
  b 2p   **e** 50p
  c 10p   **f** 1p

2 a 5p   **c** 14p
  b 8p   **d** 13p

Page 16

1 a 13 → 14   18 → 19
    26 → 27   31 → 32
  b 19 → 18   15 → 14
    26 → 25   20 → 19
  c 7 → 17   19 → 29
    14 → 24   22 → 32
  d 18 → 8   21 → 11
    32 → 22   29 → 19

2 a 5p 16p   **b** 16p 30p

Page 17

1 a   **b**

2 a 11→13, 15→17, 13→15
  b 8→10, 16→18, 20→22

Page 18

The missing numbers are in **bold**.

1 a 7, **8**, **9**, 10, 11, **12**, **13**
  b **14**, 15, **16**, **17**, 18, 19, **20**
  c 19, **18**, **17**, 16, **15**, 14, **13**
  d **15**, **14**, **13**, 12, **11**, 10, **9**

2 Check cans are joined in this order: 7p, 9p, 11p, 13p, 14p, 15p, 18p, 20p

Page 19

1 a 10 + 5   **f** 10 + 2
  b 10 + 8   **g** 10 + 4
  c 10 + 1   **h** 10 + 3
  d 10 + 6   **i** 10 + 7
  e 10 + 9

2 a thirteen   **e** twelve
  b eleven   **f** sixteen
  c nineteen   **g** seventeen
  d fourteen   **h** eighteen

Page 20

1 a Check that half of each plate is coloured.

b Check that one square is coloured.

2 a Check that loop is around four stars.

b Check that loop is around three moons.

Page 21
1 The 1st letter is A.
The 5th letter is E.
The 7th letter is G.
The 4th letter is D.
The last letter is Z.
F is the 6th letter.
C is the 3rd letter.
L is the 12th letter.
P is the 16th letter.
B is the 2nd letter.

2 a MATHS
b MAGIC

Page 22
1 a

2 Wednesday   Sunday
Saturday   Thursday
Friday   Tuesday
Monday

Page 23
1 a 12p   **c** 8p
b 30p   **d** 18p

2 Other answers are possible.
The given answers use the least number of coins.

a

b

c

Page 24
1 a	7	**f**	7	**k**	9
b	4	**g**	8	**l**	9
c	6	**h**	5	**m**	6
d	2	**i**	5	**n**	10
e	6	**j**	8	**o**	10
2 a	7	**d**	10	**g**	9
b	9	**e**	7	**h**	6
c	6	**f**	10		

Page 25
1 a 5   **c** 4   **e** 3
b 4   **d** 3   **f** 2

2 a odd one out 5 – 2
b odd one out 4 – 0
c odd one out 6 – 5

Page 26
1 a 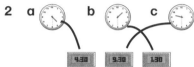 **b** **c**

2

Page 27
1 The numbers 72, 74, 76, 78, 80, 82, 84, 86, 88 and 90 should be coloured red.
a even
b odd

2 a 106, 105, 104, 103
b 92, 94, 96, 98
c 97, 99, 101, 103
d 95, 100, 105, 110
e 102, 100, 98, 96

Page 28
1 a 2   **c** 4   **e** 8
b 10   **d** 5   **f** 3

2 a 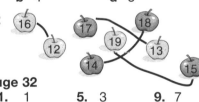 **b** **c**

9.30   9.30   1.30

Page 29
1 a 6, 7
b 8, 9
c 10, 11
d 12, 13
e 14, 15

2 a **c** **e**
b **d**

Page 30
1 a 17   **e** 20   **i** 19
b 12   **f** 1   **j** 16
c 6   **g** 12   **k** 10
d 15   **h** 3   **l** 5

2 a 5   **c** 12   **e** 5
b 3   **d** 4

Page 31
1 a 4   **c** 3
b 4   **d** 5

2 16, 12, 17, 19, 18, 14, 13, 15

Page 32
1. 1   **5.** 3   **9.** 7
2. 5   **6.** 7   **10.** 10
3. 2   **7.** 9
4. 8   **8.** 4

Page 33
1. 6   **6.** three
2. 8   **7.** nine
3. 12   **8.** eleven
4. 15   **9.** seventeen
5. 20   **10.** nineteen

Page 34
1. 9   **5.** 9   **9.** 10
2. 7   **6.** 8   **10.** 9
3. 9   **7.** 8
4. 8   **8.** 10

Page 35
1. ☐ ☑ ☐
2. ☐ ☐ ☑
3. ☑ ☐ ☐
4. ☐ ☑ ☐ ☐
5. ☐ ☐ ☐ ☑
6. ☐ ☑ ☐
7. ☑ ☐ ☐
8. ☐ ☐ ☐ ☑
9. ☐ ☑ ☐ ☐
10. ☐ ☐ ☐ ☑

Page 36
1. square   **6.** ☐
2. rectangle   **7.** △
3. triangle   **8.** ☐
4. star   **9.** ☆
5. circle   **10.** ○

Page 37
The missing numbers are in **bold**.
1. 2 3 4 **5 6**
2. **5 6** 7 8 9
3. **7 8** 9 10 **11**
4. **9** 8 7 **6 5**
5. **6** 5 4 3 **2**
6. **8 9** 10 11 12
7. **3** 4 5 **6 7**
8. 12 11 10 **9 8**
9. **8 7** 6 5 4
10. **10 9** 8 7 **6**

Page 38
1. 6   **5.** 1   **9.** 10
2. 4   **6.** 10   **10.** 10
3. 7   **7.** 10
4. 8   **8.** 10

Page 39
1. 13   **5.** 19   **9.** 9
2. 15   **6.** 13   **10.** 11
3. 15   **7.** 18
4. 20   **8.** 13

Page 40
1. 3 o'clock
2. 9 o'clock
3. 1 o'clock
4. 10 o'clock
5. 5 o'clock

6. **9.**

7. **10.**

8.

Page 41
1. straight sides
2. not straight sides
3. straight sides
4. not straight sides
5. straight sides
6. less than 10
7. not less than 10

ANSWERS

8. not less than 10
9. less than 10
10. not less than 10

Page 42
The missing numbers are in **bold**.
1. 8 9 10 **11 12 13**
2. **8 9** 10 11 12 **13**
3. **14** 15 16 17 **18 19**
4. 15 14 13 **12 11 10**
5. **12 11** 10 9 8 **7**
6. 14 15 16 **17 18 19**
7. 7 8 9 10 **11 12**
8. 20 19 18 **17 16 15**
9. **17** 16 15 14 **13 12**
10. 19 **18** 17 **16** 15 14

Page 43
1.
2.
3.
4.
5.

6. T   8. Y   10. A
7. L   9. A

Page 44
1. 5   5. 2   9. 5
2. 4   6. 2   10. 6
3. 0   7. 2
4. 8   8. 2

Page 45
1. same   6. same
2. heavier   7. lighter
3. heavier   8. heavier
4. lighter   9. same
5. lighter   10. lighter

Page 46
1. sphere   6. cuboid
2. cube   7. cone
3. cylinder   8. cube
4. cone   9. sphere
5. cuboid   10. cylinder

Page 47
1. 10   5. 12   9. 7
2. 8   6. 5   10. 7
3. 15   7. 6
4. 10   8. 4

Page 48
1. 12   5. 16   9. 8
2. 14   6. 4   10. 13
3. 15   7. 11
4. 11   8. 12

Page 49
1. 2   5. 10   9. 13
2. 6   6. 7   10. 15
3. 8   7. 11
4. 12   8. 9

Page 50
1. 3   2. 9   3. 1   4. 7   5. 4
6.   7.
8.   9.
10.

Page 51
1. 5   5. 1   9. orange
2. 4   6. vanilla   10. 19
3. 6   7. lemon
4. 3   8. mint

Page 52
The missing numbers are in **bold**.
1. 64 66 68 **70 72 74**
2. 110 108 106 **104 102 100**
3. 93 95 97 **99 101 103**
4. 75 77 79 **81 83 85**
5. 101 99 97 **95 93 91**
6. 65 70 75 **80 85 90**
7. 110 105 100 **95 90 85**
8. 90 85 80 **75 70 65**
9. 75 80 85 **90 95 100**
10. 85 90 95 **100 105 110**

Page 53
Other answers are possible.
1.   6.
2.   7.
3.   8.
4.   9.
5.   10.

Page 54
1. 3   6. 9
2. 6   7. 6
3. 2   8. 4
4. 7   9. 2
5. 1   10. 7

Page 55
1.   2.
3.   4.

5.   6.
7.   8.
9.   10.

Page 56
1. ∧   5. ⌒   9. △□•
2. ⌇   6. 1 1 2   10. 1 2 3
3. ⊓   7. ○|
4. ⌄   8. □□•

Page 57
1. 5   6. 6
2. 9   7. 10
3. 13   8. 14
4. 17   9. 18
5. 21   10. 22

Page 58
1. 1 2 4 6 8
2. 2 3 4 7 9
3. 2 4 6 9 10
4. 3 5 7 10 15
5. 5 8 9 11 17
6. 9 10 15 17 20
7. 10 11 12 14 19
8. 11 12 13 17 19
9. 13 14 15 16 20
10. 16 17 18 19 20

Page 59
1. 7   5. 6   9. 3
2. 5   6. 4   10. 4
3. 3   7. 6
4. 4   8. 3

Page 60
1. Sunday
2. Wednesday
3. Tuesday
4. Monday
5. Friday
6. Saturday
7. Monday
8. Wednesday
9. Sunday
10. Thursday

Page 61
1. III   5. IIII   9. ⦀⦀ IIII
2. II   6. ⦀⦀ I   10. ⦀⦀ I
3. ⦀⦀   7. ⦀⦀ II
4. I   8. ⦀⦀ I

English

Age 5-6

Contents

Activities

Quick Tests

Lynn Huggins-Cooper and Louis Fidge

Speaking and listening – asking questions

Are you good at listening?
Let's find out!

1 Ask a grown-up these questions. Can you remember the answers afterwards?

a What was your favourite toy when you were little?

b What was your favourite book?

c Did you have a favourite food?

d Where did you like playing?

e Who was your best friend?

2 Ask a friend these questions. Can you remember the answers afterwards?

a What do you like best about school?

b What is your favourite activity?

c What do you do at lunchtime?

d What do you play at playtime?

e What do you do after school?

Rhyming words

Look at this sentence. All the words in bold rhyme. That means the endings of the words have the **same sound**. They all end in the letters *at*.

The **fat cat sat** on the **mat**, watching a **bat!**

1 Draw a line to join each word with its rhyme partner.

a can   red

b pink   sack

c bug   dot

d bed   stink

e pot   plug

f back   fan

2 Look in the box to find words that rhyme with each word below. Write the words in the blank spaces.

a yell   _____

b dark   _____

c dog   _____

d box   _____

e win   _____

f sock   _____

g big   _____

fox
frog
dig
smell
rock
bin
park

The alphabet

a b c d e f g h i j k l m n o p q r s t u v w x y z

When words are in **alphabetical order** it means they appear in the same order as the alphabet. *A* words come first, then *b* words, right up until the end of the alphabet.

bat zebra ant put into alphabetical order is **ant bat zebra**.

1 **Write these letters in alphabetical order.**

a f b a d c e g   _____

b z x y w v u   _____

c p r q t s u v   _____

d g f i h k j m l   _____

e m l n k j o p   _____

f s t v u w r x   _____

g d f e h i g j k   _____

2 **Write each set of words in alphabetical order.**

a cat   egg   box   _____

b bag   dig   apple   _____

c cup   art   dig   _____

d car   baby   dog   _____

e wall   bed   door   _____

f book   sun   leg   _____

g tree   bird   peg   _____

Spelling simple words

Learning to spell is easy when you use:
LOOK, COVER, WRITE, CHECK.

First **look** at the word. Look to see if there are any letters with tails that hang below the line, or sticks that 'stick up' above the line. Try to see the word in your head.

tail y | stick

Then **cover** the word up and try to **write** it. Uncover the word and **check** it. See if you were right. Keep practising!

1 Learn these words. Use LOOK, COVER, WRITE, CHECK.

a saw   d yes   g was

b say   e did   h but

c now   f not   i run

2 Look at the picture and add the missing letter to each word. Use the letters in the box to help you.

a m___n 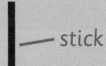   e d___t

| a |
| i |
| o |
| u |

b f___n   f w___g

c c___t   g s___n

d p___n   h b___ll

5

Writing practice

It is important to **write neatly**, so that people can read your writing. Before you start, make sure you are sitting comfortably and you are holding your pencil in the right way between your finger and thumb.

1 Trace over these words. Start at the red dot each time.

a way   us   to

b too   how   her

c him   old   one

d or   out   saw

e so   not   now

2 Copy each word three times.

a see _____ _____ _____

b ran _____ _____ _____

c our _____ _____ _____

d pot _____ _____ _____

e that _____ _____ _____

Full stops and capital letters

A sentence always **starts** with a capital letter and most sentences **end** with a full stop. The pronoun *I* is always a capital letter.

It is hot today.

/ \
capital letter   full stop

1 Rewrite these sentences, adding capital letters and full stops.

a i like you _____

b this is my sister _____

c sausages are my favourite _____

d i am going out _____

e i want to read _____

2 These sentences are mixed up. Write them out in the correct order. Use a capital letter and a full stop in each sentence.

a like brother i my

_____

b dog my walking likes

_____

c smell the cat food can its

_____

d eat we sweets

_____

e wet makes rain you

_____

Names

The name of a **person** or **place** should **start** with a capital letter.

*My cat is called **W**iggy.*

*I come from **B**righton.*

1 Circle the letters that should be capitals.

a brian

b mrs jones

c andrew

d england

e mr brown

f miss lacey

g london

h mr smith

i france

j janet

k doctor doolittle

l cambridge

m africa

n scotland

2 Now <u>underline</u> all of the letters that should be capitals in these sentences. Do not forget to add the full stops!

a my friend jamila comes from yorkshire

b my dog is called bertie

c auntie jane lives in edinburgh

d bruce, stella and jodi are my friends

e we sailed down the river thames

f dad's name is john

g i am going on holiday to portugal with my sister sarah

h i went to durham to see the pantomime cinderella

ff words

Words are made when letters and groups of letters are put together. Learning the way that groups of letters are put together helps you to **build new words**.

$$o + f = of \quad o + ff = off$$

The two *ff*s sound different to one *f* on its own.

1 Look at these letters and groups of letters. Write the words they make in the puffs of smoke.

a flu + ff =

b pu + ff =

c bu + ff =

d cu + ff =

e sni + ff =

f sti + ff =

g mu + ff =

h stu + ff =

i sta + ff =

j whi + ff =

2 Write the correct *ff* word next to each picture. Use the words in the box to help you.

| muff | cliff | giraffe | puff | whiff | sniff |

a _____

b _____

c _____

d _____

e _____

f _____

ll words

Some words end in *ll*. These letters always have a vowel in front of them.

a e i o u

tall

---

1 Make words using the endings in the ball.

a b*all bull bill bell*

b y_____

c s_____

d c_____

e h_____

all ell ill ull oll

f d_____

g f_____

h p_____

i t_____

j w_____

---

2 Write the *ll* word for each picture.

a

___ ___ ___ ___

c

___ ___ ___ ___

e

___ ___ ___ ___

b
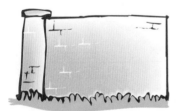

___ ___ ___ ___ ___

d

___ ___ ___ ___

f

___ ___ ___

ss and zz words

Some words end in *ss* or *zz*.

floss

buzz

1 Join the *ss* word to the right picture.

a address

b chess

c pass

d dress

e cress

f floss

2 Choose a word containing *ss* or *zz* from the box to complete each sentence.

hiss	floss	fuzzy	grass	muzzle	cress

a I sat on the _____.

b My cat's nose is soft and _____.

c I like egg and _____ sandwiches.

d Candy _____ is sweet!

e My dog wears a _____ when

she goes for a walk.

f The snake went _____.

bl words

b and *l* make the letter blend *bl*. Lots of words **start** with *bl*.

blew

bloom

1 Tick the words that start with the blend *bl*.

a back dark bland

b black bright big

c baby bin blue

d blend bark brave

e bus blank broom

f bleat bran bill

g burn bleep ball

h bloat bunny barn

i brand bit bleak

j blade brass bust

2 Draw a picture for each *bl* word. This will show that you know what it means.

a blade

c blow

e blast

b blink

d blue

ee words

The letters *ee* together sound like someone is squealing!

1 Draw a line to match each *ee* word to the right picture.

a sleep

b sheep

c feet

d sleet

e sheet

f bee

g deer

h beep

2 Draw a circle round the *ee* word in each sentence.

a The water is deep.

b Have you seen my dad?

c Where have you been?

d My sister is a teenager.

e I shall creep up the stairs, because my brother is sleeping.

f Have a peep at these chicks!

g The car horn went beep.

h In the winter we get sleet as well as snow.

oo sounds

oo makes a **special sound**, like an owl hooting.

h**oo**t r**oo**t s**oo**n

1 **Draw a picture of the missing *oo* words in the boxes below. Use the words in the box to help you.**

stool	pool	food	school

a The cat sat on the _____.

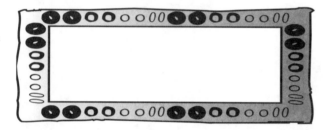

b Who would like to swim in the _____?

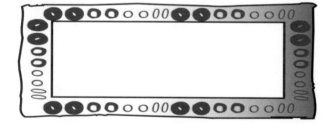

c The _____ was very noisy!

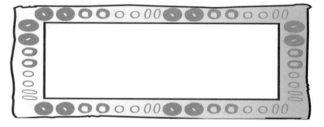

d What is your favourite _____?

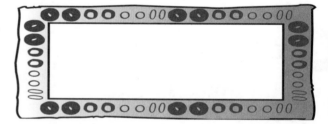

2 **Write the correct *oo* word in each sentence.**

a The _____ was bright in the sky.

b The lemonade was lovely and _____.

c I eat yoghurt with a _____.

d Can I come _____?

e _____ is made into jumpers.

too
moon
wool
cool
spoon

oa words

There are lots of words that use the letters *oa* together. They make a sound like the name of the letter *o*.

coach

toad

1 **Which pictures are *oa* words? Circle the ones you choose.**

a

b

c

d

e

f

2 **Draw a line to match each *oa* word to its clue.**

a toast   it sails on the sea

b foal   cars drive on this

c coal   bread

d loaf   baby horse

e oak   it is like a frog

f boat   it burns on a fire

g toad   a hot, cooked slice of bread

h road   tree

ai words

The letters *a* and *i* blend together to make the sound *ay* – just like a person who has not heard what you said properly!

1 **Draw a picture for each *ai* word.**

a snail

c brain

e train

b rain

d tail

f nail

2 **Write a sentence using each *ai* word.**

a snail _____

b main _____

c pail _____

d fail _____

e rain _____

f pain _____

ie and *y* words

The letter blend *ie* sometimes makes the same sound as the letter *y*, especially when it is at the end of a word – so it can be confusing!

p**ie**

wh**y**

1 Which letters are correct? <u>Underline</u> the right answer.

a pie   py

b tie   ty

c die   dy

d ly   lie

e drie   dry

f try   trie

g why   whie

h flie   fly

i cry   crie

j by   bie

2 Complete the words. They all end in *y* or *ie*.

a d_____

c cr_____

e t_____

b fl_____

d sp_____

Looking at *un*

Un is a **prefix** that can be used at the front of a word to change its meaning. A prefix is a set of letters.

un + happy = **un**happy

1 **Add the *un* to each word to make a new word.**

a un + fair = _____

b un + likely = _____

c un + aware = _____

d un + kind = _____

e un + clear = _____

f un + wanted = _____

2 <u>Underline</u> **the *un* word in each sentence.**

a Calling people names is very unkind.

b Put the unwanted clothes in that bag to go to charity.

c It is unlikely that an elephant will run across the garden!

d I think it's unfair that I have to do the dishes.

e Fighting with my sister makes me unhappy.

Commas

Commas help us to make sense of the things we read.

When you are reading aloud, commas help you to know when to take a pause.

The cat went into the garden, but then she changed her mind and came straight back!

1 **Put the commas in these sentences.**

a I like oranges best but I also like apples.

b Would you like this book or would you prefer that one?

c When we get to the shop would you like to buy a cookie?

d Hamsters are my favourite animal but I also love cats.

e I'd like a biscuit but I'd prefer a cake.

2 **Finish these sentences.**

a The cat scratched at the window, _____

b It is raining, _____

c The spider crawled up the wall, _____

d I wanted some chocolate, _____

e I saw a shooting star, _____

Exclamation marks

Exclamation marks show strong feelings, such as excitement and shock.

The dog knocked me over!

1 Add the exclamation marks to these sentences.

a I hate cabbage

b I love chocolate cake

c This is the best birthday I have ever had

d What a great book

e Ouch That really hurt

f That was such fun

2 Write sentences that end in exclamation marks. Remember, they show strong feelings.

a _____

b _____

c _____

d _____

e _____

f _____

Using *er*, *est*, *ed* and *ing*

Suffixes are sets of letters that can be added to the end of a word to make a different word.

fast ➡ fast**er** ➡ fast**est**

1 Add *er* and *est* to these words to make new words.

a slow ➡ _____ _____

b quick ➡ _____ _____

c long ➡ _____ _____

d short ➡ _____ _____

e tall ➡ _____ _____

f strong ➡ _____ _____

2 Choose the suffix *ed* or *ing* to make sure these sentences make sense.

a The cat jump_____ off the chair.

b It is rain_____.

c The baby laugh_____ when she saw the teddy.

d The mouse keeps squeak_____.

e The sunflower is grow_____ very tall.

f The duck was quack_____ at the chicken.

Spelling the days of the week

Monday **Tuesday** **Wednesday**

Thursday **Friday** **Saturday** **Sunday**

1 **Learn these spellings. Use LOOK, COVER, WRITE, CHECK.**

a Monday _____

b Tuesday _____

c Wednesday _____

d Thursday _____

e Friday _____

f Saturday _____

g Sunday _____

2 **Fill in the missing letters to spell the days of the week.**

a Mo_____ _____ay

b Sat_____ _____ _____ay

c T_____u_____s_____a_____

d Tu_____ _____ _____ay

e We_____ _____es_____ _____ _____

f Su_____ _____ _____y

g Fr_____ _____ _____y

Plurals

With some words, to change from one thing to more than one thing (a **plural**) you just add an *s*.

With some words you add *es*.

wish ➡ wish**es**

cat ➡ cat**s**

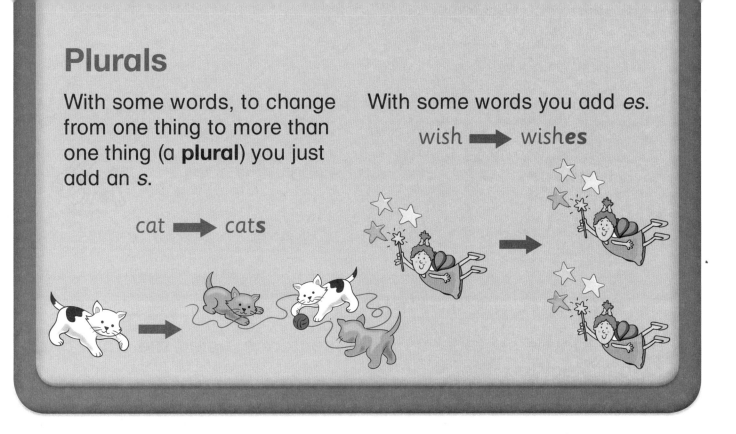

1 Change these words to plurals.

a rabbit ➡ _____

b dog ➡ _____

c cow ➡ _____

d horse ➡ _____

e chicken ➡ _____

f duck ➡ _____

2 Change these words to plurals.

a fox ➡ _____

b dish ➡ _____

c class ➡ _____

d kiss ➡ _____

e princess ➡ _____

f dress ➡ _____

Using *and*

You can join simple sentences by using the word *and*.

The bunny hopped up the garden. It ate some grass.

↓

The bunny hopped up the garden, **and** it ate some grass.

1 Rewrite these sentences as one sentence, using the word *and* to join them together.

a A moth flew near the window. It patted the glass with its wings.

_____

b My mum likes cake. She likes biscuits.

_____

c My teddy is big. He has long fur.

_____

d The wizard waved his wand. The cat turned into a tiger!

_____

e The cake is chocolate flavour. It has creamy icing.

_____

2 Draw a line to join the two parts of the sentences together so they make sense.

a I like reading books   1 and a sandpit in the park.

b I like lollies   2 and I like ice cream!

c I went to London   3 and a dog.

d I have a cat   4 and a skateboard.

e There is a swing   5 and watching films.

f I have a bike   6 and to Brighton.

Contractions

When you see a word like *I'm*, it is called a **contraction**. The apostrophe shows that letters are missing.

I'm didn't she's

1 **Draw a line to join the words to their contractions.**

a will not   he's

b shall not   won't

c I have   I've

d can not   shan't

e he has   can't

2 **Change these words to their contractions.**

a did not   ➡ _____

b had not   ➡ _____

c have not ➡ _____

d I would   ➡ _____

e do not   ➡ _____

25

Making words

You can **build words** by adding different groups of letters together.

cr + **isp** = *crisp*

---

1 Add these groups of letters together and write the words you make. The first one has been done for you.

a th + at = <u>that</u>

b th + is = _____

c th + en = _____

d wh + at = _____

e wh + en = _____

f wh + ip = _____

g tr + ap = _____

h dr + op = _____

i cr + op = _____

j br + an = _____

---

2 Join together the groups of letters with a line to make words. Use a different colour felt pen for each word.

a tr   ant

b pl   ade

c br   ing

d bl   it

e cr   en

f sm   ab

g spl   esh

h dr   ile

i fr   ip

j wh   ee

Syllables

Syllables are the sounds that make up words.

badger is made up of **badg + er**

1) How many syllables are there in each of these animal words? Say the words out loud to help you. Write the number of syllables in the box.

a fox

b robin

c spider

d hedgehog

e squirrel

2) Break each word into syllables. The first one has been done for you.

a raining ➡ ___rain/ing___

b sunshine ➡ _____

c windy ➡ _____

d snowing ➡ _____

e thundering ➡ _____

In the past

When the **action word** in a sentence ends in *ed* it means the action happened in the past.

I walk**ed** to school yesterday.

1 Change the action word to the past tense. The first one has been done for you.

a I enjoy_ed_ the games best.

b I talk_____ to my friend.

c I look_____ at the picture.

d She play_____ with her brother.

e He paint_____ a picture.

f I call_____ my sister.

g They wash_____ their hands.

2 Write the correct present tense word next to the past tense word. The first one has been done for you.

a jumped   _jump_

b laughed   _____

c enjoyed   _____

d called   _____

e guessed   _____

f lifted   _____

g watched   _____

h worked   _____

i helped   _____

| watch | jump | laugh | help |
| enjoy | guess | call | work | lift |

Vowels

The letters

a e i o u

are called **vowels**.

Sometimes *y* acts as a vowel in words like *cry* and *why*.

Do have some tea.

1 Circle the vowels in these words.

a cottage

b seaside

c woods

d babies

e school

f computer

g picture

h doctor

i berries

j leaf

2 Fill in the missing vowels to make these words.

a h_____ _____se

c gl_____ss_____s

e c_____k_____

b b_____ _____ks

d m_____lk

f st_____rs

Consonants

Consonants are all the letters of the alphabet except the vowels *a e i o u*.

The consonants are:

b c d f g h j k l m n p q r s
t v w x y z

---

1 <u>Underline</u> the consonants in these words.

a boat

b baby

c mouse

d sand

e sunshine

f desk

g pencil

h scissors

i envelope

j table

---

2 Write the names of the things under the pictures. Use pairs of consonants in the box to help you.

a

___ a ___

c

___ e ___

e

___ a ___

b

___ a ___

d

___ a ___

ct lg mn

jm cn

Question marks

Question marks look like this **?** They are used at the end of a sentence to show it is a question.

Some words give us a clue that a question is being asked:

What...? When...? How...? Why...? Who...?

Where is my hat?

1 Add a question mark or a full stop at the end of these sentences.

a Do you like football

b I am glad we are going there

c Can we go now

d May I have one please

e You can play

f This is my dog

g What was that noise

h What time is it

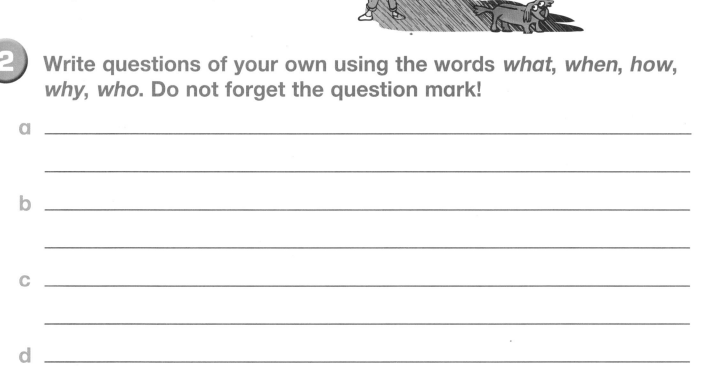

2 Write questions of your own using the words *what*, *when*, *how*, *why*, *who*. Do not forget the question mark!

a _____

_____

b _____

_____

c _____

_____

d _____

_____

e _____

_____

Test 1 The alphabet

All **words** are made up of **letters**. There are **26** letters in the **alphabet**.

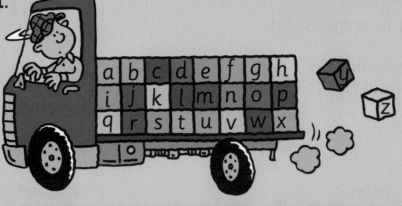

Fill in the missing letters.

Colour in your score

Test 2 Making some words (1)

The sound of the **first letter** of each of these words is the **same**.

sun   saw   sink

Choose one of these letters to start each word.

m   p   h

1. ___eg

2. ___an

3. ___op

4. ___in

5. ___at

6. ___ut

7. ___en

8. ___op

9. ___ug

10. ___en

Colour in your score

Test 3 Making some words (2)

We use **letters** to make **words**.

b + a + t = bat

Do these sums. Write the words you make.

1. s + a + d = _____

2. d + i + g = _____

3. b + a + g = _____

4. t + o + p = _____

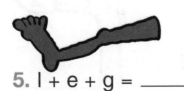

5. l + e + g = _____

6. f + o + x = _____

7. n + e + t = _____

8. t + u + b = _____

9. d + o + g = _____

10. j + u + g = _____

10
9
8
7
6
5
4
3
2
1

Colour in your score

Test 4 Labels

Many pictures have **labels** to help you.

eye

ear

nose

whiskers

tail

leg

Write the correct name under each animal.

| monkey | goat | horse | tiger | kangaroo |
| donkey | bear | zebra | camel | panda |

1. _____

2. _____

3. _____

4. _____

5. _____

6. _____

7. _____

8. _____

9. _____

10. _____

10

9

8

7

6

5

4

3

2

1

Colour in your score

Test 5 **Sentences**

A **sentence** must make **sense**.

I to hop like. ☒   I like to hop. ☑

Write the words in order to make some sentences.

1. sun yellow. The is _____

2. green. is grass The _____

3. read. like to I _____

4. lay eggs. Hens _____

5. lion A roar. can _____

6. raining. is It _____

7. in You water. swim _____

8. ball. You a kick _____

9. door The shut. is _____

10. stripes. A has tiger _____

10
9
8
7
6
5
4
3
2
1

Colour in your score

36

Test 6 Missing words

A **sentence** must make **sense**.

A roars. ☒   A lion roars. ☑

Choose the best word to finish each sentence.

| elephant | sun | money | cup | kangaroo |
| banana | star | spade | bike | umbrella |

1. You ride a _____.

2. The _____ shines.

3. A _____ twinkles.

4. You spend _____.

5. You eat a _____.

6. A _____ hops.

7. You need an _____ in the rain.

8. You drink from a _____.

9. An _____ has a trunk.

10. You dig with a _____.

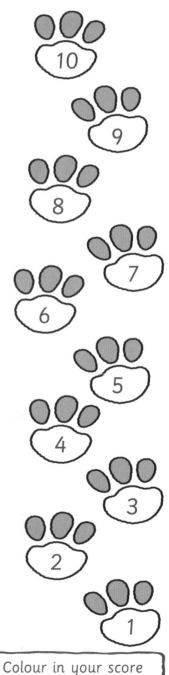

Colour in your score

37

Test 7 **Last letters**

The sound of the **last letter** of each of these words is the **same**.

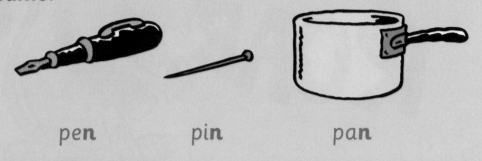

pen   pin   pan

Choose one of these letters to finish each word.

t   g   p

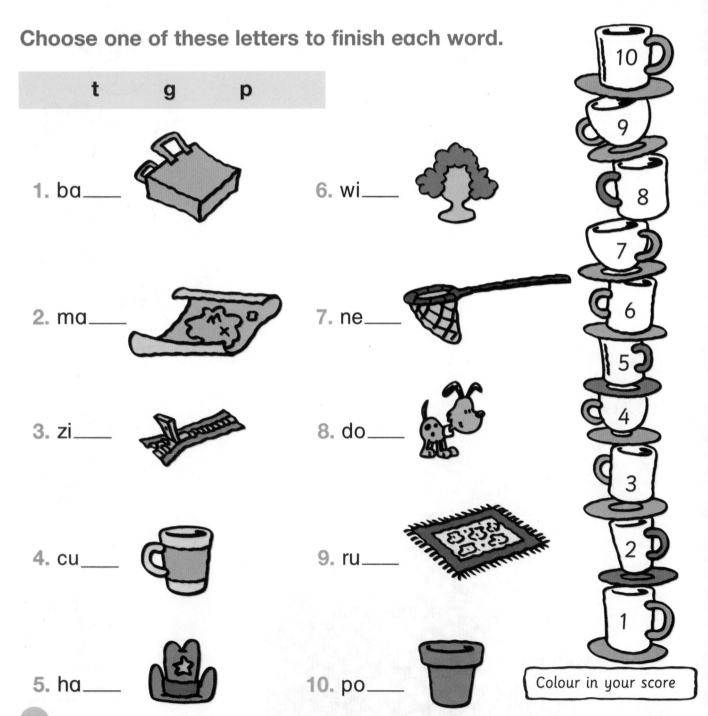

1. ba___

2. ma___

3. zi___

4. cu___

5. ha___

6. wi___

7. ne___

8. do___

9. ru___

10. po___

Colour in your score

38

Test 8 Groups of words

We sometimes **group** words together. These are all **birds**.

hen   parrot   sparrow

bike   rocket   helicopter   bus   aeroplane

boat   yacht   car   ship   lorry

Sort these things into groups.

Things that go on land.

1. _____	3. _____
2. _____	4. _____

Things that fly in the sky.

5. _____
6. _____
7. _____

Things that go on the water.

8. _____
9. _____
10. _____

10

9

8

7

6

5

4

3

2

1

Colour in your score

39

Test 9 Word building

We can **build** words from **letters** and **groups of letters**.

b + ag

bag

r + ag

rag

w + ag

wag

Do these sums. Write the words you make.

1. f + an = _____

6. r + od = _____

6

2. s + ix = _____

7. p + eg = _____

3. v + an = _____

8. c + ut = _____

4. n + od = _____

9. m + ix = _____

5. l + eg = _____

10. n + ut = _____

Colour in your score

40

Test 10 Middle letters

The sound of the **middle letter** of each of these words is the **same**.

pan   bat   bag

Choose the correct middle letter to make each word.

a o 1. j__m	o i 6. s__b
u a 2. t__p	i e **10** 7. t__n
u o 3. l__g	e i 8. t__n
o u 4. b__n	a i 9. b__b
u e 5. t__b	e a 10. j__t

10
9
8
7
6
5
4
3
2
1

Colour in your score

41

Test 11 Capital letters and full stops

A **sentence** always begins with a **capital letter** and often ends with a **full stop**.

The girl fell off her bike!

Write these sentences correctly.

1. the rain falls _____

2. a tree grows tall _____

3. the sky is blue _____

4. my cup is full _____

5. a cow moos _____

6. we like books _____

7. you bang a drum _____

8. it is sunny _____

9. a ball is round _____

10. i like to sing _____

10
9
8
7
6
5
4
3
2
1

Colour in your score

Test 12 **The letters *ff, ll, zz* and *ss***

Some words end with **double letters**.

Pass the ba**ll**.

	doll		off		bell	
hill		buzz		puff		fall
	hiss		fuzz		fuss	

Write the words that end with *ss*.

1. _____   2. _____

Write the words that end with *ll*.

3. _____   5. _____

4. _____   6. _____

Write the words that end with *zz*.

7. _____   8. _____

Write the words that end with *ff*.

9. _____   10. _____

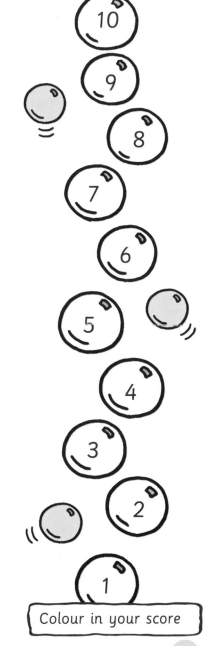

Colour in your score

43

Test 13 The letters *ck* and *tch*

Many words end in *ck* or *tch*.

A du**ck** says qua**ck**.

The wi**tch** has an i**tch**.

Do these sums. Write the words you make.

1. b + a + ck = _____

2. p + a + ck = _____

3. n + e + ck = _____

4. p + e + ck = _____

5. k + i + ck = _____

6. st + i + tch = _____

7. w + a + tch = _____

8. b + a + tch _____

9. w + i + tch = _____

10. f + e + tch + _____

10

9

8

7

6

5

4

3

2

1

Colour in your score

44

Test 14 The letters *ng* and *nk*

Many words end in *ng* and *nk*.

I can si**ng**.

I can thi**nk**.

Find and write the *ng* or *nk* words that are hiding.

1. a (b a n g) w   *bang*

2. b a n k t y   _____

3. h g k i n g   _____

4. b s o n g m   _____

5. f v s a n k   _____

6. h a n g j b   _____

7. s a r i n g   _____

8. z l i n k n   _____

9. b u n k x c   _____

10. j h p i n k   _____

Colour in your score

Test 15 Letter blends at the beginning of words

These words all have *l* as a second letter.

slide   fly   clock   black   glue

Write the new words you make.

1. Change the **fl** in **fl**ip to **sl**. _slip_

2. Change the **pl** in **pl**ot to **sl**. _____

3. Change the **sl** in **sl**at to **fl**. _____

4. Change the **cl** in **cl**ick to **fl**. _____

5. Change the **fl** in **fl**ap to **cl**. _____

6. Change the **bl** in **bl**ink to **cl**. _____

7. Change the **cl** in **cl**ot to **bl**. _____

8. Change the **sl** in **sl**ack to **bl**. _____

9. Change the **cl** in **cl**ass to **gl**. _____

10. Change the **cl** in **cl**ad to **gl**. _____

Colour in your score

Test 16 Letter blends at the end of words

Say these words slowly. Listen to the way they **end**.

bolt   she**lf** mi**lk** he**lp**   go**ld**

	hold	elf	milk	
yelp	belt	silk	gold
	help	shelf	melt	

Write the pairs of rhyming words.

Write the words that end with *ld*.

1. _____ 2. _____

Write the words that end with *lf*.

3. _____ 4. _____

Write the words that end with *lk*.

5. _____ 6. _____

Write the words that end with *lp*.

7. _____ 8. _____

Write the words that end with *lt*.

9. _____ 10. _____

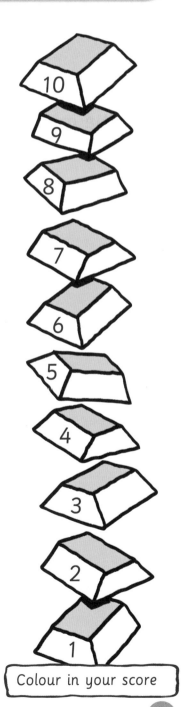

10
9
8
7
6
5
4
3
2
1
Colour in your score

Test 17 Plurals

Plural means when there is **more than one**.

We add *s* to many words to make them plural.

one rabbit

three rabbits

Fill in the missing word.

1. one hat but two _____

2. one leg but two _____

3. one tin but two _____

4. one pot but two _____

5. one mug but two _____

6. one _____ but two pans

7. one _____ but two pets

8. one _____ but two lips

9. one _____ but two dogs

10. one _____ but two sums

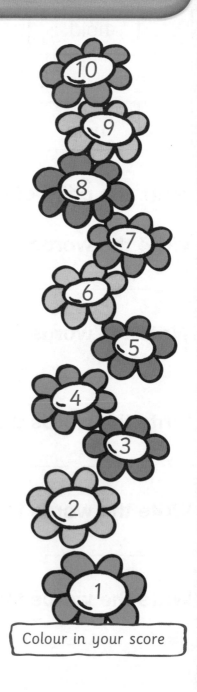

Colour in your score

48

Test 18 Sets of words

This is a **set** of fruit.

orange banana apple

This is a **set** of animals.

lion   monkey   elephant

potato   butterfly cabbage onion   ant

carrot   beetle   cauliflower earwig   turnip

Write the names of the vegetables.

1. _____   4. _____

2. _____   5. _____

3. _____   6. _____

Write the names of the insects.

7. _____   9. _____

8. _____   10. _____

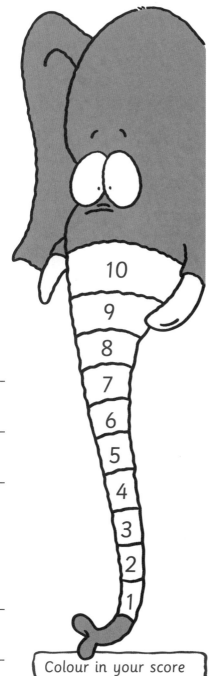

10
9
8
7
6
5
4
3
2
1

Colour in your score

49

Test 19 Silly sentences

A **sentence** must make **sense**.

The dog moos. ⊠   The dog barks. ☑

Change the last word so that each sentence makes sense. Choose words from the box to help you.

barks   moos   hisses   cheeps   neighs
chirps   quacks   bleats   brays   buzzes

1. A cow barks. _____

2. A dog moos. _____

3. A duck hisses. _____

4. A horse cheeps. _____

5. A hen neighs. _____

6. A sheep chirps. _____

7. A snake quacks. _____

8. A bird bleats. _____

9. A bee brays. _____

10. A donkey buzzes. _____

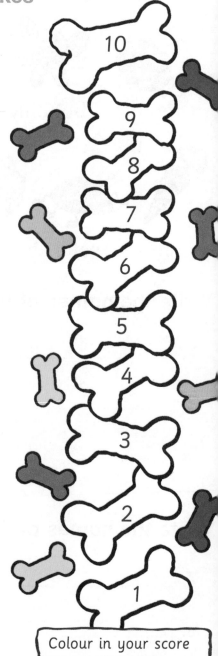

Colour in your score

50

Test 20 The letters *sh* and *ch*

You will find *sh* and *ch* in many words.

fi**sh** and **ch**ips

Choose *sh* or *ch* to complete each word.

1. _____est

2. _____ell

3. _____ip

4. di_____

5. _____eep

6. ben_____

7. _____icken

8. tor_____

9. _____eese

10. bru_____

Colour in your score

51

Test 21 The letters *ee* and *oo*

The letters *ee* and *oo* are two common letter patterns.

*I have some b**oo**ts on my f**ee**t.*

Choose *ee* or *oo* to complete each word.

1. _____l

2. st_____l

3. p_____l

4. br_____m

5. m_____n

6. tr_____

7. w_____p

8. f_____d

9. sw_____t

10. b_____

Colour in your score

Test 22 The letters *ay* and *ai*

The letters *ay* often come at the **end** of a word.

The letters *ai* often come in the **middle** of a word.

tr**ay**

tr**ai**n

Choose *ai* or *ay* to complete the word in each sentence.

1. It is a lovely d_____.

2. The r_____n is falling.

3. I hit the n_____l with a hammer.

4. You can swim in the b_____.

5. You can make things with cl_____.

6. The sn_____l went slowly.

7. I had to w_____t for my dinner.

8. You can pl_____ in the park.

9. The plates are on a tr_____.

10. You will have to w_____t and see.

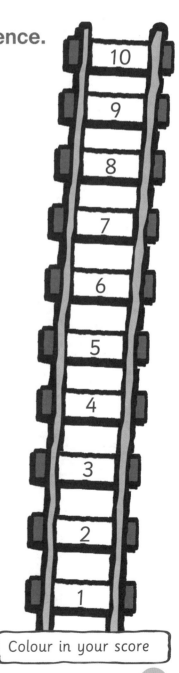

10
9
8
7
6
5
4
3
2
1

Colour in your score

Test 23 Vowels and consonants

There are **26** letters in the **alphabet**.

a	b	c	d	e	f	g	h	i	j	k	l	m
n	o	p	q	r	s	t	u	v	w	x	y	z

The five **vowels** are *a, e, i, o, u*.

All the other letters are called **consonants**.

Fill in the missing letter in each word.

1. m___t

2. s___n

3. b___d

4. ___et

5. b___b

6. b___g

7. fo___

8. s___x

9. m___d

10. bu___

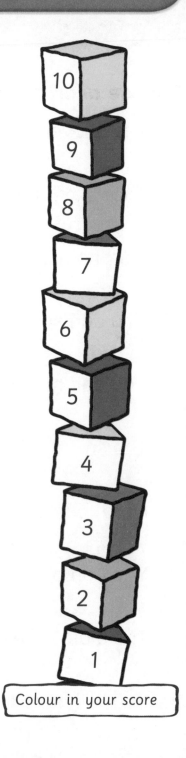

10
9
8
7
6
5
4
3
2
1

Colour in your score

54

Test 24 **Names**

Whenever we write **someone's name** we should always **start** with a **capital letter**.

Humpty **D**umpty sat on a wall.

Write the names of these nursery rhyme characters correctly.

1. humpty dumpty _____

2. little bo peep _____

3. margery daw _____

4. tommy tucker _____

5. jack horner _____

6. polly _____

7. mary _____

8. lucy locket _____

9. georgie porgie _____

10. bobby shafto _____

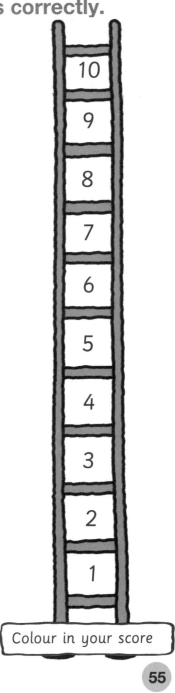

10
9
8
7
6
5
4
3
2
1

Colour in your score

Test 25 The endings *ing* and *ed*

We can add *ing* and *ed* to the ends of some words.

I am wash**ing** my face.
wash + ing = washing

Yesterday I wash**ed** my feet.
wash + ed = washed

Add *ing* to each word. Write the word you make.

1. talk _____

2. lick _____

3. draw _____

Add *ed* to each word. Write the word you make.

4. shout _____

5. kick _____

6. crawl _____

Take the *ing* off. Write the word you are left with.

7. sniffing _____

8. sleeping _____

Take the *ed* off. Write the word you are left with.

9. turned _____

10. passed _____

Colour in your score

56

Test 26 **Questions**

A question must begin with a **capital letter** and end with a **question mark**.

capital letter
question mark

How many legs has a spider?

Write these questions correctly.

1. what is for tea

   _____

2. when are you coming

   _____

3. what shape is a ball

   _____

4. who is making that noise

   _____

5. where do you live

   _____

6. how many sweets have you got

   _____

7. what is your address

   _____

8. who is your teacher

   _____

9. when is it time for dinner

   _____

10. where is London

   _____

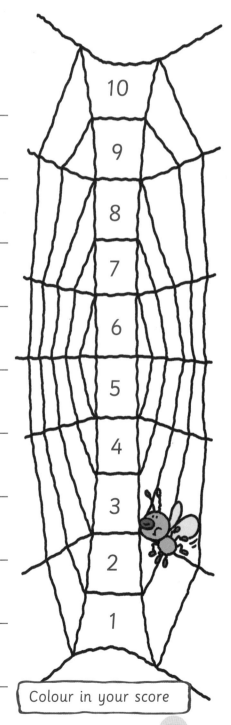

10
9
8
7
6
5
4
3
2
1

Colour in your score

Test 27 The letters *ea* and *oa*

The two letter patterns *ea* and *oa* are common.

*a b**oa**t on the s**ea***

Write the new words you make.

1. Change the **s** in **s**ea to **t**. _____

2. Change the **b** in **b**eat to **s**. _____

3. Change the **l** in **l**eap to **h**. _____

4. Change the **b** in **b**eak to **l**. _____

5. Change the **t** in **t**each to **b**. _____

6. Change the **g** in **g**oat to **b**. _____

7. Change the **f** in **f**oal to **g**. _____

8. Change the **t** in **t**oad to **r**. _____

9. Change the **c** in **c**oast to **t**. _____

10. Change the **p** in **p**oach to **c**. _____

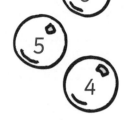

10
9
8
7
6
5
4
3
2
1

Colour in your score

58

Test 28 Magic *e*

Look what happens when we add *e* to the **end** of some words.

hop + e = hop**e**

Do these sums. Write the words you make.

1. mad + e = _____

2. slid + e = _____

3. plan + e = _____

4. can + e = _____

5. cub + e = _____

6. rob + e = _____

7. shin + e = _____

8. cut + e = _____

9. tap + e = _____

10. bit + e = _____

Colour in your score

Test 29 The months of the year

It is important to know how to spell the **months of the year** correctly.

Here are the months of the year in the wrong order.

August	May	December	January
February	June	October	March
September	April	November	July

Fill in the missing months in order. Spell them correctly.

The first two months have been done for you.

January

February

1. _____

2. _____

3. _____

4. _____

5. _____

6. _____

7. _____

8. _____

9. _____

10. _____

Colour in your score

10 9 8 7 6 5 4 3 2 1

Test 30 Rhyming

Sometimes words that rhyme use the same spelling pattern.

A plane can **fly** in the **sky**.

	ring	bake	train	
goat	cool		king	coat
	chain	pool	cake	

Write the pairs of rhyming words.

Write the *ing* words.

1. _____

2. _____

Write the *ool* words.

3. _____

4. _____

Write the *oat* words.

5. _____

6. _____

Write the *ain* words.

7. _____

8. _____

Write the *ake* words.

9. _____

10. _____

Colour in your score

61

ANSWERS

Page 2
1. Make sure your child can ask the questions successfully, and can remember the answers afterwards.
2. Make sure your child can ask the questions successfully, and can remember their friend's answers afterwards.

Page 3
1. a fan   d red
   b stink   e dot
   c plug   f sack
2. a smell   e bin
   b park   f rock
   c frog   g dig
   d fox

Page 4
1. a a b c d e f g
   b u v w x y z
   c p q r s t u v
   d f g h i j k l m
   e j k l m n o p
   f r s t u v w x
   g d e f g h i j k
2. a box, cat, egg
   b apple, bag, dig
   c art, cup, dig
   d baby, car, dog
   e bed, door, wall
   f book, leg, sun
   g bird, peg, tree

Page 5
1. Spellings remembered.
2. a man
   b fan/fin/fun
   c cat/cot/cut
   d pan/pin/pun
   e dot
   f wag/wig
   g sin/son/sun
   h ball/bill/bull

Page 6
1. Words overwritten neatly.
2. Words copied correctly; rounded letters, correctly formed, sitting on lines.

Page 7
1. a I like you.
   b This is my sister.
   c Sausages are my favourite.
   d I am going out.
   e I want to read.

2. a I like my brother.
   b My dog likes walking.
   c The cat can smell its food.
   d We eat sweets.
   e Rain makes you wet.

Page 8
1. a (B)rian
   b (M)rs (J)ones
   c (A)ndrew
   d (E)ngland
   e (M)r (B)rown
   f (M)iss (L)acey
   g (L)ondon
   h (M)r (S)mith
   i (F)rance
   j (J)anet
   k (D)octor (D)oolittle
   l (C)ambridge
   m (A)frica
   n (S)cotland

2. a <u>M</u>y friend <u>J</u>amila comes from <u>Y</u>orkshire.
   b <u>M</u>y dog is called <u>B</u>ertie.
   c <u>A</u>untie <u>J</u>ane lives in <u>E</u>dinburgh.
   d <u>B</u>ruce, <u>S</u>tella and <u>J</u>odi are my friends.
   e <u>W</u>e sailed down the <u>R</u>iver <u>T</u>hames.
   f <u>D</u>ad's name is <u>J</u>ohn.
   g <u>I</u> am going on holiday to <u>P</u>ortugal with my sister <u>S</u>arah.
   h <u>I</u> went to <u>D</u>urham to see the pantomime <u>C</u>inderella.

Page 9
1. a fluff   f stiff
   b puff   g muff
   c buff   h stuff
   d cuff   i staff
   e sniff   j whiff
2. a giraffe d whiff
   b puff   e cliff
   c sniff   f muff

Page 10
1. Children will not know all of the words below, but they are given for correctness.
   a ball, bull, bill, bell
   b yell
   c sill, sell
   d call, cell, cull

   e hill, hall, hull, hell
   f doll, dell, dull, dill
   g fall, fill, full, fell
   h pull, pill, pall, poll
   i till, tall, tell, toll
   j will, wall, well
2. a ball   d bull
   b wall   e well
   c bell   f doll

Page 11
1.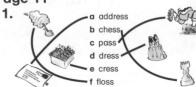
   a address
   b chess
   c pass
   d dress
   e cress
   f floss
2. a grass   d floss
   b fuzzy   e muzzle
   c cress   f hiss

Page 12
1. a bland f bleat
   b black   g bleep
   c blue   h bloat
   d blend   i bleak
   e blank   j blade
2. Check child's pictures of the words listed.

Page 13
1.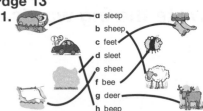
   a sleep
   b sheep
   c feet
   d sleet
   e sheet
   f bee
   g deer
   h beep
2. a deep
   b seen
   c been
   d teenager
   e creep, sleeping
   f peep
   g beep
   h sleet

Page 14
1. Pictures of the items mentioned:
   a stool   c school
   b pool   d food
2. a moon   d too
   b cool   e Wool
   c spoon

Page 15

1. Circled: a, d, e, f

2. **a** a hot, cooked slice of bread
   b baby horse
   c it burns on a fire
   d bread
   e tree
   f it sails on the sea
   g it is like a frog
   h cars drive on this

Page 16

1. Check child's pictures of the items listed.

2. Sentences using the words listed.

Page 17

1. **a** pie **e** dry **h** fly
   b tie **f** try **i** cry
   c die **g** why **j** by
   d lie

2. **a** die **c** cry **e** tie
   b fly **d** spy

Page 18

1. **a** unfair **d** unkind
   b unlikely **e** unclear
   c unaware **f** unwanted

2. **a** unkind **d** unfair
   b unwanted **e** unhappy
   c unlikely

Page 19

1. **a** I like oranges best, but I also like apples.
   b Would you like this book, or would you prefer that one?
   c When we get to the shop, would you like to buy a cookie?
   d Hamsters are my favourite animal, but I also love cats.
   e I'd like a biscuit, but I'd prefer a cake.

2. Any sensible, meaningful sentence endings.

Page 20

1. Talk to your child about why there are exclamation marks at the end of each sentence.

2. Any sensible sentences that end in exclamation marks. Again, talk to your child about why exclamation marks need to be included.

Page 21

1. **a** slower, slowest
   b quicker, quickest
   c longer, longest
   d shorter, shortest
   e taller, tallest
   f stronger, strongest

2. **a** jumped **d** squeaking
   b raining **e** growing
   c laughed **f** quacking

Page 22

1. Check your child has learnt the correct spellings.

2. **a** Monday **e** Wednesday
   b Saturday **f** Sunday
   c Thursday **g** Friday
   d Tuesday

Page 23

1. **a** rabbits **d** horses
   b dogs **e** chickens
   c cows **f** ducks

2. **a** foxes **d** kisses
   b dishes **e** princesses
   c classes **f** dresses

Page 24

1. **a** A moth flew near the window, and it patted the glass with its wings.
   b My mum likes cake, and she likes biscuits.
   c My teddy is big, and he has long fur.
   d The wizard waved his wand, and the cat turned into a tiger!
   e The cake is chocolate flavour, and it has creamy icing.

2. **a** 5 **c** 6 **e** 1
   b 2 **d** 3 **f** 4

Page 25

1. **a** won't **d** can't
   b shan't **e** he's
   c I've

2. **a** didn't **d** I'd
   b hadn't **e** don't
   c haven't

Page 26

1. **a** that **f** whip
   b this **g** trap
   c then **h** drop
   d what **i** crop
   e when **j** bran

2. Words created using word beginnings and endings.
   a trade, trip, tree
   b plant
   c bring

   d blade, blab, blip (bling, if the child knows this word)
   e crab
   f smile
   g split
   h drab, drip
   i fresh, free
   j when, while, whip, whee

Page 27

1. **a** 1 **c** 2 **e** 2
   b 2 **d** 2

2. **a** rain/ing **d** snow/ing
   b sun/shine **e** thun/der/ing
   c win/dy

Page 28

1. **a** enjoyed **e** painted
   b talked **f** called
   c looked **g** washed
   d played

2. **a** jump **f** lift
   b laugh **g** watch
   c enjoy **h** work
   d call **i** help
   e guess

Page 29

1. **a** c(o)t t(a)g(e)
   b s(e)(a)s(i)d(e)
   c w(o)(o)d s
   d b(a)b(ie)s
   e s c h(o)(o)l
   f c(o)m p(u)t(e)r
   g p(i)c t(u)r(e)
   h d(o)c t(o)r
   i b(e)r r(ie)s
   j l(e)(a)f

2. **a** house **d** milk
   b books **e** cake
   c glasses **f** stars

Page 30

1. **a** boat **f** desk
   b baby **g** pencil
   c mouse **h** scissors
   d sand **i** envelope
   e sunshine **j** table

2. **a** cat **c** leg **e** man
   b jam **d** can

Page 31

1. **a** ? **d** ? **g** ?
   b . **e** . **h** ?
   c ? **f** .

2. Questions written using the question words provided.

ANSWERS

Page 32
1. c
2. g
3. i
4. m
5. p
6. s
7. t
8. v
9. x
10. z

Page 33
1. peg
2. pan
3. hop
4. pin
5. mat
6. hut
7. hen
8. mop
9. mug
10. pen

Page 34
1. sad
2. dig
3. bag
4. top
5. leg
6. fox
7. net
8. tub
9. dog
10. jug

Page 35
1. camel
2. horse
3. kangaroo
4. zebra
5. bear
6. tiger
7. monkey
8. goat
9. donkey
10. panda

Page 36
1. The sun is yellow.
2. The grass is green.
3. I like to read.
4. Hens lay eggs.
5. A lion can roar.
6. It is raining.
7. You swim in water.
8. You kick a ball.
9. The door is shut.
10. A tiger has stripes.

Page 37
1. bike
2. sun
3. star
4. money
5. banana
6. kangaroo
7. umbrella
8. cup
9. elephant
10. spade

Page 38
1. bag
2. map
3. zip
4. cup
5. hat
6. wig
7. net
8. dog
9. rug
10. pot

Page 39
Answers 1–4, 5–7, 8–10 can be given in any order.
1. bike
2. bus
3. car
4. lorry
5. rocket
6. helicopter
7. aeroplane
8. boat
9. yacht
10. ship

Page 40
1. fan
2. six
3. van
4. nod
5. leg
6. rod
7. peg
8. cut
9. mix
10. nut

Page 41
1. jam
2. tap
3. log
4. bun
5. tub
6. sob
7. ten
8. tin
9. bib
10. jet

Page 42
1. The rain falls.
2. A tree grows tall.
3. The sky is blue.
4. My cup is full.
5. A cow moos.
6. We like books.
7. You bang a drum.
8. It is sunny.
9. A ball is round.
10. I like to sing.

Page 43
Answers 1–2, 3–6, 7–8, 9–10 can be given in any order.
1. hiss
2. fuss
3. doll
4. bell
5. hill
6. fall
7. buzz
8. fuzz
9. off
10. puff

Page 44
1. back
2. pack
3. neck
4. peck
5. kick
6. stitch
7. watch
8. batch
9. witch
10. fetch

Page 45
1. bang
2. bank
3. king
4. song
5. sank
6. hang
7. ring
8. link
9. bunk
10. pink